THE MODERN FARM HEN

BY

CHESLA C. SHERLOCK

Published by
THE HOMESTEAD COMPANY
Des Moines, Iowa

Copyrighted 1922 by

THE HOMESTEAD COMPANY

All rights reserved.

New Edition 2021 by

The Ages Publishing

To my father,
WALLACE E. SHERLOCK,
who first had faith in me
and from whom I have inherited
a profession.

PREFACE

A few farmers have recognized the fine profit to be made from the production of high-class market eggs and the sale of hatching eggs and baby chicks in the breeding season. They have laid out the farm poultry work so that it can be efficiently handled in connection with general farming. And they are making good money.

The thought has been with the author for some years that the methods used by these progressive men and women, if placed in a form accessible to other farmers, should do much towards elevating the general standard of the farm hen and would make farm poultry generally more profitable.

The result has been the bringing together of this book which is written entirely for farmers and is based upon the experience and the methods of actual farmers. It deals only from the practical standpoint, keeping ever in mind the units and the conditions best adapted for average farm conditions. It attempts to reduce into a formula, as much as possible, every step along the road to poultry success.

It should answer many of the questions which people are constantly raising as to the possibilities in poultry for the farmer. It will answer questions of methods, procedure and means. It exists for no other purpose.

Grateful acknowledgment is made to Dante M. Pierce, who has made this work possible.

Des Moines, Iowa.   Chesla C. Sherlock.

TABLE OF CONTENTS

PREFACE
CHAPTER I
What Farm Poultry Raisers Are Doing..1
Egg Farming On a Commercial Scale by Farmers...............................2
Making Poultry a Profitable Side-line..3
What Actual Farm Men and Women of the Middle West Are Doing..4
D. E. Carlson, Iowa..5
Mrs. Etta Bechtel, Iowa..8
Hugo Anderson, Minnesota...10

CHAPTER II
A Practical Farm Flock Unit..13
Capital and Ground Necessary for Best Results.................................14
How to Determine the Size of the Flock...17
Reducing Labor and Overhead to a Minimum by Proper Planning..19

CHAPTER III.
The Selection of Breeds...23
The Breeds of Economic Value to the Farmer...................................24
How TO Select the Breed to Fit the Purpose in Mind......................26
The Meaning of Strains and Their Value...30

CHAPTER IV
Buildings and Equipment for the Flocks..33
Missouri Fool-Proof House..35
The Minnesota Type House...37
The Lord Farms Small Flock House..40
Colony Houses, Brooding Houses and Coops...................................42
Colony Brooder Coop for 100 Chicks...43
Coal Burning Brooder House..44
Semi-Monitor Colony Coops...45
Range Boosting Coop...45
Small Flock Breeding House..46

Two-Pen Small Flock Breeding Coop..46
Nests, Hoppers and Appliances..47
Trap Nests...49
Hoppers and Feed Boxes..49

CHAPTER V
The Laws and Principles of Breeding..53
Heredity...54
Variation..55
Reversion...56
Prepotency...56
Line-Breeding..57
Inbreeding...61
Cross-Breeding..62
Grading Up the Flock...62
Selecting the Breeding Stock...64

CHAPTER VI
Care of the Farm Flock Breeding Pen..67
Feeding for Fertile Eggs...69
Selection and Care of Hatching Eggs..70
Fertility and Hatchability op Eggs..72
Trap-Nesting and Pedigreeing...75

CHAPTER VII
Natural and Artificial Incubation...77
The Modern Incubator fob Hatching...78
How TO Handle the Incubator..80
Mammoth Incubators and Their Management..................................84
Running a Hatchery..86

CHAPTER VIII
Successful Brooding of Chicks...89
FIRELESS Brooders..91
Oil Lamp Brooders...92
Crude Oil Brooders...94
Portable Coal Hover Brooders...95
Brooder House Methods...96

Care of Chicks on Large Scale..97

CHAPTER IX
How to Feed Poultry of All Ages..99
Value of Rations..101
First Feeding of Baby Chicks..101
Feeding Baby Chicks to Feather Them Out.......................................104
From Three to Eight Weeks..104
Two Months to Maturity..105
Feeding for Market...106
Feeding the Laying Flock..107
Dry Mash..110
Scratch Feed..110
Feeding the Breeders..113

CHAPTER X
Developing the Young Stock Properly....................................115
Value and Kinds of Range..117
Rations and Methods...119

CHAPTER XI
Culling Farm Poultry for Any Purpose..................................123
Purposes of Culling..124
Culling Young Stock..125
Fall Culling of Pullets...126
Culling the Layers..129
External Characteristics of Good Layers..132

CHAPTER XII
Care and Management for "Winter Eggs"...........................139
Regularity In Caring for the Flock..141
Keeping Things Clean..142
Should the Layers Have Range?...143

CHAPTER XIII
Artificial Lighting for Winter Eggs..145
Results..147
Costs...148
Systems One Mat Use..149

How TO Run Lights..149
Dangers and Pitfalls to Avoid..150
Automatic Regulation of Lights..151

CHAPTER XIV
Marketing Farm Eggs Successfully..153
How TO Pack for Shipment..155
About Marking..156
Express Classification Rules..157
Use of Cartons..158
Grading Eggs..159
Private Trade..161
Advertising...162

CHAPTER XV
How to Sell and Advertise Stock...165
How TO Pack and Ship Hatching Eggs....................................166
Where and How to Advertise..168

CHAPTER XVI
Poultry Diseases and Remedies...175
Roup..177
Diphtheria...178
Chicken Pox..179
Cholera...179
Typhoid..180
White Diarrhoea...180
Tuberculosis..181
Intestinal Worms..181
Limberneck...182
Scaly Legs...183
Lice, Mites..183

ILLUSTRATIONS

A Portion of an Iowa Farmer's Side-line Poultry Plant......................6

Plant Built Up by an Iowa Farm Woman..9

Small Farm Poultry Plant Housing 250 Laying Hens......................11

A Practical Flock of 500 Layers Maintained by a Farmers Wife....15

Young Stock on Range..18

A Farm Poultry House Built of Hollow Building Tile....................20

Single Comb White Leghorn Hen...24

White Wyandotte Hen...25

Single Comb Rhode Island Red Hen..26

Columbian Plymouth Rock Hen...27

Barred Plymouth Rock Pullet..29

Iowa Semi-Monitor Type Laying House..33

Cross-section of Iowa Semi-Monitor House....................................34

Floor Plan of one unit of Pen. Iowa Semi-Monitor House.............35

A Row of Missouri Fool-Proof Poultry Houses..............................36

Front Elevation, Missouri Fool-Proof House..................................36

Fool-Proof Shutter Adapted to Colony Coop...................................37

An Adaptation of the Minnesota Laying House..............................39

Front Elevation Lord Farms Small Flock Laying House................40

Cross-section Lord Farms Small Flock Laying House...................41

Colony Coop for 100 Baby Chicks...42

Front Elevation Coal Burning Brooder House................................43

Cross-section Coal Burning Brooder House...................................44

Semi-Monitor Colony Coop Used by Charles Laros......................45

Range Roosting Coop..45

Small Flock Breeding Houses...46

Two- Pen Small Flock Breeding Coop....................................46

Rear Wall Ventilating Device of Fig. 27..................................47

Showing Interior Arrangement of Fig. 27...............................47

One Method of Construction to Save Space.......................48

Darkened Nest Compartment for Wall Use.........................49

Simple Wall Nest...49

For Nests Under Dropping Board (Side View).....................50

Another View of Nests to Go Under Dropping Board........50

Cornell Trap-Nest...51

Missouri Trap Nest...52

Lord Farms Large Flock Hopper...52

These Fine White Rocks Are the Result of Proper Breeding..........53

Line-breeding Tends to Secure Uniformity...........................55

This Chart Makes It Easy to Follow Line Breeding.............60

A Desirable Type of Sire to Head the Breeding Pen..........61

Chart Showing Increase of Pure-blood Through Grading..............63

Which would you select to head the breeding pen?..........64

A Farm Flock Breeding Pen Where Mass Breeding Is Followed...68

Ideal Quarters for Breeding Pen...71

An Excellent Breeding Pen of White Wyandottes..............75

Outside Runs for Chicks in the Brooder House...................90

Hollow Tile Brooder House on a Dallas County, Iowa, Farm........94

Colony Brooder House With Small Run................................97

Proper Rations and Systematic Care..................................100

Young Stock Being Fed for Early Maturity..........................102

Five-months-old pullet...106

The Importance of Plenty of Fresh Water..112

Colony Houses With Good Range..116

An Economical Roosting Coop for Young Stock.........................118

A Colony Coop in the Orchard..120

High-producing Leghorns, having record of 288 and 269 eggs....124

Showing Desirable Head on Good Layer..128

The Small, Snaky Head on Undesirable Layers............................129

Showing Desirable Abdominal Capacity for a Heavy Layer........131

Pubic Bone Test—a "Three-Finger" Hen.......................................134

A "Two-Finger" Layer..136

Line Shows Increase in Egg Production...146

Simple Alarm Clock Arrangement..151

Egg Cartons Containing Your Farm Name Build Up a Demand..155

Carefully Selected Eggs Ready for Shipment................................158

Grade the Eggs Carefully for the Best Price..................................162

Roadside Signs Will Attract Attention to Your Farm....................166

One Way of Advertising Your Products...167

CHAPTER I

What Farm Poultry Raisers Are Doing

Opportunities In Poultry Farming— Egg Farming On a Commercial Scale by Farmers— Making Poultry a Profitable Side-Line— What Actual Farm Men and Women of the Middle West Are Doing

Interest in farm poultry was never greater than at the present time. This interest has steadily increased during the past twenty years, due to the rapid strides made in scientific feeding, breeding, culling and in the development of successful methods of housing the flock. The close attention paid to breeding, the development of the 200-egg laying hen, the perfection of the incubator and of brooding devices whereby large flocks of young chicks might be handled at one operation, have all played a tremendous part in the fostering of proper interest on the farm in poultry culture.

It is doubtless true that the greatest incentive has come through the failure of other farm products to measure up to the high level of price stability attained and maintained year after year by poultry and poultry products. Hens properly cared for and fed have always been profitable, regardless of existing price levels and in recent years they have been more profitable than any other farm product.

The opportunities in poultry farming were never more promising. We do not, at the present time, in spite of our great production of eggs and market poultry, produce sufficient stocks to support our own needs. Thousands of cases of Chinese and Danish eggs are shipped into this country every season. Then, again, the American egg supply comes largely from the farm hen, which means that the production largely occurs during the summer months and that the great percentage of the supply must go into storage to meet the winter demand. People do not like storage eggs and they will pay a premium for fresh eggs rather than eat them. This means that the farmer or commercial poultryman who masters his

1

craft and learns how to secure winter eggs will be in an unusually favorable position to secure the highest prices of the season and the greatest profit from his labor and investment.

Modern housing methods, modern feeding and the practice of artificial lighting have all aided greatly in making winter egg production a matter-of-fact proposition to the man who cares to exert himself along the proper line. For the expenditure of a comparatively slight sum for "seed" stock, the mere novice can secure the work of years of the best utility breeders in the world, thereby starting in with heavy egg-laying strains, where others commenced with mere nondescript layers.

Egg Farming On a Commercial Scale by Farmers

The farmer is in a peculiarly favorable position to engage in egg farming on a serious scale. He has the land, the soil, the range. He is in a position to grow practically all of the necessary feed right upon his place. If he carries a good-sized flock of laying hens as a side-line, he has the added advantage of feeding his feed upon his own place, thereby turning an additional profit from it.

The business of egg farming is primarily adapted to the farm. While great profits are made by many small poultrymen with limited acreage and range, the maximum of profit will undoubtedly be found to be in favor of the farmer. His land is not so high in value; he has less of an investment to take into consideration; he has more land and, therefore, a greater choice of location for his various duties in connection with the poultry business. Last, but not least, his overhead will be slightly greater than it now is under the present system of general farming.

More farmers should engage in egg farming on a commercial scale because of the opportunities it offers for a profitable market for the farm-grown grain and produce. Poultry make the greatest spread of profit and the quickest turn-over of any form of live-stock farming. Where the live stock breeder is required to wait six months, one year, or even two years, for a return on the grain and feed consumed, the poultryman waits but a few days for returns on the feed consumed by laying hens. He can produce an entire new unit (hen) within six months of feeding, whereas it would take more than a year to produce almost any other form of live stock. Where the hen consumes 75 to 90 pounds of feed during a producing year, a dairy cow will consume that amount several times in a year and perhaps not net as much profit as one hen.

The rapidity with which the feed fed into poultry will secure a cash return, the comparatively short time in which the working units are replaced, the slight capital involved in any one unit, and the fact that hens are the most efficient users of the feed consumed, all combine to make commercial egg farming of interest to farmers, from the production standpoint.

There is another element to consider. The busy seasons with the poultry comes at times when the average farmer generally has little to do outside of the usual "chores." During the winter, general farm work is comparatively light. That is the period of greatest activity for the scientific egg farmer. In the spring, the majority of the chicks can be hatched and brought to the point where they are able to largely take care of themselves before the general rush of spring farm work sets in. Through the summer, if they have range and are handled under the colony system and are hopper-fed, they will require a minimum of attention from the farmer. They commence to require close attention in the fall when the harvest is completed on the average farm, releasing the farmer from the bulk of his year's work.

Making Poultry a Profitable Side-line

Where it is not possible, or considered advisable, to engage in commercial egg farming on an extensive scale, or as the main purpose in life, the farmer is still in a splendid position to develop egg farming up to the extent of his possibilities, as a side-line. Many farmers in the Middle West are carrying as large flocks as a sideline to other farming activities, as many commercial egg farmers are able to carry. This is due to the fact that they have recognized the extreme value of equipment, proper housing, proper methods of care and feeding and have arranged everything with the idea of making every motion count for the most. We shall mention a few of these people a little later in this chapter.

Poultry is adapted to side-line purposes on the average farm for the same reason that it can desirably be made the chief concern, where other specialized interests do not interfere. Poultry farming in connection with live stock breeding has been carried on successfully by a number of Corn Belt farmers and breeders. It is a success on general farms, on fruit farms, on waste land, on poor land, on high-priced land. There is not a single specialized kind of farming that poultry will not fit into with the possible exception of truck farming and, then, there are many points of contact between these two that might make them advantageous to each other.

A number of Iowa farm men and women are regularly carrying 1,000 laying hens as a side-line to some other kind of farm work. They are enabled to do this because they have taken a leaf from the experience of the commercial egg farmers and have availed themselves of every advantage gained through the experience of these men. They have provided the proper types of houses for their birds for their climate, they have studied the principles of breeding and have applied them, they have studied rations and the feeding properties of grains and feeds— in short, they have not permitted the laying hen to shift for herself, but have set about the work of intelligently giving her the advantage of the best poultry experience the world has to offer. And they have succeeded, as the records plainly show.

There is no particular "secret" about the business of making poultry a profitable side-line to general farming or present farming work. It takes no particular brand of luck with poultry there is but slight element of risk in it now, with methods so largely standardized, indeed, less than in the production of most farm crops. The hustler, the worker, the man who is thorough in his work and who does not become lazy or indifferent, the man who is willing to learn and to apply the results of the experiments made by others when it will benefit him, is the type of man who will succeed.

What Actual Farm Men and Women of the Middle West Are Doing

It is a singular fact that very few of the men and women of the Middle West who have made a success of poultry farming voluntarily took up that work. Some outside force, some grim necessity, seems to have been the moving cause of their first serious attention to egg farming.

But thousands of farmers are now seriously interested in the possibilities of poultry farming. They are making a careful study of the situation; they are talking to and interviewing poultry raisers in all parts of the country they are asking the advice of their farm and poultry journals, and are visiting more or less successful poultry plants in their own neighborhood and are taking short courses at their state college preparatory to engaging in the work on a more or less extensive scale.

Back of it all there lurks that individual interest in the success of others, for it gives us all something to pin our faith to. Can we succeed? Will we succeed? How can we be sure of success? How did those who are a success start? These and numerous other questions suggest themselves to the beginner.

We have attempted to indicate briefly the personal experience of several outstanding men and women in the poultry business on the farm in the Middle West so as to answer these questions. The experiences of many more people might have been given, but they would serve no useful purpose, no purpose not met in the experiences given herewith.

One fact has been impressed strongly upon the author and that is that the success of practically every person he has ever interviewed who has won at poultry farming has been grounded upon the same identical factors, namely, proper foundation stock, proper housing, proper care and feeding, plus attention to details. That is all there is to poultry success. We leave it to the reader.

D. E. Carlson, Iowa.

D. E. Carlson, an Iowa farmer who farms 115 acres of land, has made a big success from egg farming as a side-line to general farm work. Several years ago he was taking in $4,000 per year from his flock of 1,000 layers. He is doubtless doing better than that at the present time, as he has since increased his capacity.

The story of Mr. Carlson's achievements with his poultry flock does not read with any of the sensational glamour which one finds in many stories of poultry success. It is a simple, straight-forward story of hard-headed thinking and wise planning to put the flock on a paying basis. Mr. Carlson, like most farmers, had definite ideas as to the improvements which he wished to make on his farm. In order to get at the work a little at a time and when he could afford it, he adopted the plan of making some sort of permanent improvement each year. A few years ago, it came the "turn" of the poultry to be considered.

Mr. Carlson knew that the flock needed a better house, if he was to get any sort of returns from it during the winter months when prices were high. He was in doubt as to what sort of a house would be best for general farm work. He did not take a chance and build the first thing that came along, or pick out a plan that seemed all right because someone else had it. He got on the train and went down to the agricultural college at Ames and enlisted the aid of Professor Lapp in the poultry extension department. Professor Lapp immediately recommended the semi-monitor type house, sometimes referred to as the "Iowa house," for Mr. Carlson's use. It is designed especially for the farm flock and may be used for any size or age of poultry.

Mr. Carlson returned home and built one of these houses 24x60 feet that same fall. Three hundred and seventy-five hens were placed in this house in the early part of November and during the month of December $350 worth of eggs were sold from this flock and 225 other hens kept in the old houses.

He found that the hens in the new house laid from six to eight eggs each more than those in the old house, and that settled the matter for him then and there. He determined to increase the quarters so that it

Fig. 1—A Portion of an Iowa Farmer's Side-line Poultry Plant.

would be possible for him to accommodate 1,000 layers during the winter season.

The following year an addition was built to the laying house, making it 24x96 feet and containing a feed room at one end, with feed bins, mash mixers, and a place to grade and pack the eggs. Since that time Mr. Carlson has increased his plant to include another house of this type 24x127 feet. This gives Mr. Carlson just the sort of equipment that a farm the size he maintains can support in comfortable fashion. It is necessary to buy but very little of the feed used. Mr. Carlson mixes his own mashes, grinds most of the ingredients going into them, and outside of a

CHAPTER I

few feeds necessary to start off the baby chicks and growing stock properly, everything fed is raised right on the farm.

Mr. Carlson tested the English and the American strains of Single Comb White Leghorns side by side in order to determine just which strain he wanted to use in breeding up his flock to a state of high egg production.

"I found that the American strain had it all over the English," he said. "My American Leghorns lay a large egg. In fact, I have taken prizes and secured premiums on my eggs shipped to the New York market because of their size. So I think I will stick to the American Leghorn, for in my own case it has proved to be the best producer, both in size of eggs and in number."

Mr. Carlson has a mammoth incubator which brings off hatches of several hundred eggs at one setting. This enables him to get all the young stock he needs ordinarily in one or two settings and he has the balance of the season to produce baby chicks to sell to others.

The young stock is brooded in small colony coops and brooder houses each 10x12 feet in size. These houses are built either on the semi-monitor or shed-roof type. As soon as the chicks are feathered and are able to take care of themselves, they are given range and from that time on the element of care necessary to bring them to maturity is not so great.

Mr. Carlson's success has been swift and sure. This has been due in a large measure to the fact that he sought the aid of the experts at the state agricultural station and has had the benefit of their guidance and aid ever since.

He has practiced the rigid culling necessary to weed out the drones in a flock the size he maintains. He was especially careful to have every detail right in the beginning. His housing appliances are correct in principle. His feeding rations are correct in ingredients to make heavy egg production possible.

In addition, he keeps pace with the newer developments in poultry culture. He has installed artificial lighting in the laying houses and has used the lights for several seasons with marked success. "The lights are a great aid in getting winter eggs," he said. "There can be no doubt about that." Mr. Carlson is also using trapnests for the purpose of spotting the better laying hens and pullets.

"I find that chickens require a lot of work and close attention," he said, "but they certainly make you the money. And the fine thing about it is that it is a quick cash return, something not possible with all forms of farm work."

The Carlson success is merely the result of three things: Proper housing, proper feeding and care, and attention to details. It is something within the reach of every farmer.

Mrs. Etta Bechtel, Iowa.

Mrs. Etta Bechtel, an Iowa farm woman, was forced to turn to commercial poultry production as the only way in which to earn a living for her family. The Bechtel's had become involved in an unfortunate land deal which deprived them of all of their farm land with the exception of 55 acres. They would have lost it all had Mrs. Bechtel not refused to sign the deed for the 55 acres mentioned,

"When we came back," said Mrs. Bechtel, "I determined to go into the poultry business on a large scale. I had faith in the hens and I told my husband that poultry was the only hope for salvation on the 55 acres, and he was so utterly discouraged that he agreed with me. That was eight years ago,"

Mrs. Bechtel tested out practically every breed and strain of poultry before she finally settled upon the English strain White Leghorns. Mrs. Bechtel, unlike D. E. Carlson, found that the English Leghorns laid better for her than the American strains, so all others were discarded.

"I started with 200 pullets," she continued, "and had good success from the start. I had eggs to sell and got my start by advertising in leading farm and poultry papers. I had a great business from the start in hatching eggs and have always had to turn down business through inability to supply the demand."

The market eggs produced by the Bechtels are all shipped to a commission house in New York City. During the hatching season, the output of the Bechtel plant is marketed in the form of hatching eggs and baby chicks all over the country.

"The cornerstone of my success," she said, "is based upon the fact that we started with the very best foundation stock that we could buy. When we started with the Barron strain, I bought the very best pen that we could afford. We have often paid $50 and $75 for cockerels to head our breeding pens— pedigreed birds coming from high-producing dams. At other times we have paid as high as $5 per egg for eggs coming from laying contest winners with high official records. One cannot be niggardly in this respect. The best that money can buy is the least that one can afford in this respect."

The Bechtel flock is trapnested and line-breeding for egg production is carefully carried out. They keep their hens through the second year and then dispose of them for breeding stock at from $2 to $2.50 each. The surplus cockerels from the early hatches are marketed as broilers on the New York City market. Last spring they brought 60 cents per pound when they averaged one and one-half to two pounds each.

Fig. 2—Plant Built Up by an Iowa Farm Woman.

An example of what can be done under average farm conditions in the way of winter egg records under proper environment is shown in the performance of 400 pullets on the Bechtel farm during December, 1921. These pullets netted Mrs. Bechtel $100 per week during that month, the eggs selling at 70 cents, 75 cents, 80 cents and 85 cents per dozen during the month on the New York City market. It cost Mrs. Bechtel $3.81 express to ship two cases of eggs to New York and she netted $20 per case on her eggs.

Mrs. Bechtel grades her eggs to weight and size, establishing 26 ounces to the dozen as her standard or minimum grade. Her yearling hens will produce eggs averaging around 30 ounces to the dozen. Her baby chicks are likewise carefully graded before being shipped out. This insures customer satisfaction.

Missouri fool-proof type laying and breeding houses are used on the farm, after testing them in comparison with other types, including the Iowa semi-monitor house. They found the latter was not as successful as the former, in their own case. Great consideration is given to the mating of the breeding pens, as it is one of the tests of success in poultry culture, particularly so in increasing egg production from year to year.

In 1921, Mrs. Bechtel shipped 40,000 to 50,000 baby chicks. She has a mammoth incubator of 7,000-egg capacity and several smaller 300-egg machines. Her total capacity is 10,000 eggs at one setting.

Artificial lighting and rigid culling is practiced. The Bechtels are enthusiastic in their support of artificial lighting. "When we turned on our lights," they said, "our egg production jumped 30 per cent."

Mrs. Bechtel is just an ordinary country woman, of average ability and temperament. But she has a quiet determination, an air of conviction without undue self assertiveness about her, which impresses one with the thought that she is capable of her job and entitled to the success that has come to her.

Hugo Anderson, Minnesota.

Hugo Anderson has demonstrated in a big way what can be accomplished through a small beginning in commercial egg farming. He carries a minimum of 3,500 layers through the winter each year on his 26-acre plant near Duluth, Minnesota. He has also demonstrated that cheap lands unsuited for other agricultural purposes can be made to earn a high return when turned to poultry and egg production. Mr. Anderson markets all of his eggs in privately marked cartons through a large department store in Duluth and has never been able to supply the demand.

During the hatching season he markets thousands upon thousands of baby chicks and hatching eggs all over the country. His total annual business is above the $25,000 mark, the monthly income running from $2,000 to $5,000 the year around.

Mr. Anderson is the father of the commercial egg farming community at Barnum and the largest individual producer. When he started in 1907, the hen was a curiosity in his section of the country. People had always thought that it would be impossible to keep hens that far north in the winters experienced there. There is plenty of room for this assumption when one considers that it often gets as cold as 40 degrees below zero and stays there for six weeks at a time.

Today Barnum is said to be the second largest community egg-producing center in the United States, ranking next to Petaluma, California, in this respect. Hardly a soul in Barnum is not engaged in egg production on the side. Even the cashier of the local bank has his flock of 1,000 layers on the side. At the time we visited Barnum, he was topping the list at the local creamery for the size of the egg check (Mr. Anderson does not market through the creamery, but independently) running between $600 and $700 per month.

Fig. 3—Small Farm Poultry Plant Housing 250 Laying Hens Under Ideal Conditions.

Mr. Anderson has paid close attention to egg-laying ability and has built up a high-record strain. One flock of 200 selected pullets averaged well over the 200-egg mark for him in 1918, and he states that his selected flock of layers averages 60 per cent egg production throughout the year. These records seem exceptional to breeders farther south, but when it is taken into consideration that the crisp climate in northern Minnesota tends to cut down the normal molting periods and hurries the hens to quick feather development when they do molt, it is not unreasonable.

Mr. Anderson uses artificial lighting for his layers and states that he could not get along without it. He is also severe in his culling methods and is constantly working for high flock averages, believing that is more important than individual records. He feeds correct rations, gives particular attention to the construction of his houses, as is mentioned in the chapter on Buildings, and pays close attention to details. These factors have won success for him, as they have for others.

CHAPTER II

A Practical Farm Flock Unit

How Many Hens?— Capital and Ground Necessary for Best Results— How to Determine Size of Flock—Reducing Labor and Overhead to a Minimum BY Proper Planning

The first question that comes to every farmer who wishes to give the hens the place they deserve in his farming business is, How many hens should I be able to handle at a profit? The average person is inclined to think in terms of numbers rather than in terms of profit and, consequently, overestimate the maximum sized flock that he should handle.

It is not numbers that makes for profit in the poultry business, any more than numbers make for profit with dairy cattle. The laying hen is an individual and her performance must be considered and judged as such. Many farmers are maintaining flocks of several hundred hens and are receiving such returns as they do get from a few dozen hens. It is obvious that the culls and drones deprive such farmers of profits, rather than produce them.

It is likewise possible to overdo the matter in the initial start made. The tendency too often is to seek to acquire a large flock of hens in as short a time as possible. Consequently, the beginner makes the mistake of spreading his money over numbers rather than restricting it to quality in the seed stock purchased.

No man can determine in advance just how many hens he can handle at a profit. He may estimate, but the difficulty with estimates is that they are generally overdone. The best practice, and the safest practice is to make a modest beginning with the best seed stock one can afford, then gradually expand as one learns the elements of modern methods and how to apply them to the flock. Having won a profit with the few hens, then it is in order to expand and increase the operations. This plan insures the laying of a sound foundation under your work in future years, but if you make the mistake of trying to jump into the poultry business on a full fledged scale within a year or two, you are very likely to wake up some morning and discover that you, have built the roof to your house and have given no thought to the foundation and the structure.

Make haste slowly is the best and safest rule for the beginner to follow. The farmer may think that he knows a great deal about chickens and how to handle them, but he will find, if he is fair-minded and willing to learn what has been done in the poultry world in recent years, that he has to unlearn a great deal that he already knows, and learn a lot of new practices and methods in addition.

The very best way to start is to buy a breeding pen (one male and four females) of the very best blood lines in your chosen breed that you can afford to buy. This means, in the first place, that considerable time will be spent in investigating the breeds and the strains within these breeds. After the best strain has been selected, it is then necessary to secure the very best specimens that you can afford to buy. Of course, this breeding pen will call for more of an initial outlay than baby chicks or hatching eggs would cost, but it is the safest and best plan in the long run.

For one thing, you know absolutely what you are getting, and can tell fairly well what to expect from the birds as breeders by a careful examination of them.

With hatching eggs and baby chicks the gamble is greater, and the results seldom as satisfactory. In our judgment, a breeding pen of the very highest type we could find for seed stock would well be worth $100, and it may be that you will have to pay more than that. This is not an outrageous price when you stop to consider that live stock breeders pay into the thousands of dollars for a single breeding animal which may not return any greater percentage of profit than a good laying hen. The point is that the best that money will buy is none too good for seed stock.

Capital and Ground Necessary for Best Results

The farmer will not, of course, require the capital to engage in poultry farming that anyone else would require because he has land with which to make the start. This generally eats up a good share of the commercial poultryman's capital at the outset and reduces his chances of success.

CHAPTER II

From the standpoint of capital, the farmer is in the most favorable position of anyone to engage in poultry farming. He not only has the land with which to work, but he also has practically all of his living and household expenses accounted for. This means that he can start on the proper scale for less money than the man who enters poultry farming from some other occupation.

The capital required will vary in individual cases and according to the object the farmer has in mind. In practically every case the purchase of new seed stock— pure-bred stock— will be necessary. Likewise, modern poultry buildings will have to be erected in order to prepare for the new flock. If the business is to be built up from a single pen of seed stock, no outlay will ordinarily be required for brooder houses or incubators the first season, but these must be planned for before the flock has been brought to its maximum size.

Some farmers will require practically no capital at all, outside of the money invested in seed stock. By a few well-chosen alterations in existing poultry houses on the farm, in the light of recommendations given elsewhere in this book, they can adjust the housing problem to the proper basis. Being owners of their land, no capital will be required in that direc-

Fig. 4—A Practical Flock of 500 Layers Maintained by a Farmers Wife.

tion and the general farm work can be depended upon to support them until the poultry business comes into its own, or performs its rightful share as a flourishing side-line.

To others more capital will be necessary. The existing poultry houses will have to be torn down absolutely and complete new houses constructed. This will require capital before the new flocks can be expected to produce an income. Seed stock will require capital, provision will have to be made for the brooding and shelter of the growing stock, appliances and equipment will have to be purchased or made. And the capital required will rise in amount in proportion to size of the flock which the farmer expects to maintain ultimately, because it will be necessary, in the interests of ultimate economy, to plan all building operations with this goal in mind, to look to the future and to anticipate the future wants in order to avoid a waste or loss of capital and labor. This will call for the expenditure of more capital for the time being than might otherwise be the case.

The actual amount necessary will depend upon circumstances surrounding each case. One should have, roughly speaking, sufficient capital to invest to carry him and the flock through the first full year at least. This depends upon the size of flock one may be able to carry through the first winter, and that can never be estimated to a certainty. But any flock, regardless of size, should be made to earn a profit after the first season or one might as well abandon any thought of making a success at poultry farming and turn to something else. And this is just as true where poultry is to be a side-line as where it is to be the main source of income. If it is not an efficient side-line it has no excuse for existence; it is merely eating up feed and labor that could be expended in some other direction.

It will not ordinarily be necessary for the general farmer to set aside any considerable amount of ground for the exclusive use of the poultry flock. If the proper laying houses are constructed, as recommended elsewhere in this book, no yards will be necessary at all. In fact, the laying hens will do much better from every standpoint if they are confined throughout the laying season in the laying houses. The actual ground occupied by the laying house or houses will not be a considerable item. Thousands of hens have been maintained successfully on a few acres where intensive methods are followed. In fact, where the soil is suitable for intensive poultry culture, 2,000 laying hens to the acre have been successfully produced and maintained year in and year out. There is no need for the average farmer going to this extreme; indeed, it would be practically an impossibility unless outside labor was engaged to aid in the work.

CHAPTER II

Some yardage will be necessary for the brooder houses where the chicks can be allowed to run in nice weather. But chicks are usually taken out of the brooder houses when a month to six weeks old and sent to the colony houses on range. These may be located either in the orchard or along the cornfield, thereby utilizing to double purpose land engaged in some other productive purposes.

How to Determine the Size of the Flock

There are several ways in which one can determine the size of the flock which he can best maintain, but the matter must, in the last analysis, be settled by the individual himself. The determination of the question is grounded in the purpose to which poultry is to be put, and the ability, energy and resources of the individual.

Where poultry farming is to become the chief business of the farmer, it might be said that there is no limit to which one may go. "When it is considered that many specialty breeders on comparatively small farms are doing a business annually running from $25,000 to $100,000 the truth of this statement is better appreciated. A number of large specialty breeders devote the entire acreage to poultry farming; several we have in mind, so utilizing farms over 100 acres in extent.

Looked at from a labor standpoint, one man can easily manage a flock of 1,000 layers, raise the young stock each year, run the incubators, pack and ship the eggs, as a side-line to general farming. But, and this is where the rub lies, everything must be planned and arranged, as indicated in a subsequent paragraph, so that every motion will count and all labor will be reduced to a minimum.

Practical farmers who are raising poultry as a sideline on farms in the Corn Belt have told us that they can handle 1,000 layers to good advantage without being tied down too close, and they are men who speak from experience. But they are utilizing every bit of modern equipment that will aid them in their work and they are "on their toes" all the time and on the lookout for methods to reduce their labor, eliminate lost motion, save steps, and, at the same time, not neglect the welfare of their

Fig. 5—Young Stock on Range Along Edge of Young Orchard on an Iowa Farm.

flocks.

Where poultry is to be managed as a side-line to other farm work, we have taken particular pains to determine what would be a practical rule to apply regarding the size of the flock to be maintained and have come to the conclusion, where the farm is not too large to be managed by one man successfully, that 10 hens to the acre is about all that can be handled efficiently. Again, this implies that the poultry department will be so arranged and the flock so housed as to make every move count in their care. A farm of 160 acres would give, under this rule, a flock of say 1,600 laying hens. This is the maximum that can be carried as a side-line. If it gets beyond that point it will soon be crowding the other farm work, and a flock of this size improperly handled will crowd any man, as it is. But an energetic farmer and his good wife can, under proper surroundings, maintain a sideline flock under this rule practically the entire year without additional labor.

An 80-acre farm should support 800 fowls on a sideline basis and 120 acres 1,200 layers. Flocks ranging from 500 to 1500 layers will be found to be the most efficient for average market egg production on a sideline basis, and will be sufficient to provide work for the farmer during the seasons of the year when his general farm work demands the least of his attention. At any rate, the 10 hens to the acre rule, is probably as safe an arbitrary rule as can be given. It is well to keep it in mind when one is apt to indulge in overestimates and feel the urge to try and do too much. If one organizes the work and handles flocks of the sizes indicated, for profit, not for numbers, the greatest pleasure and profit will be returned by the hens.

Reducing Labor and Overhead to a Minimum by Proper Planning

It is well to devote some time with a pencil and a pad of paper to "figuring" how one can reduce labor and overhead to a minimum in advance of the actual launching of the poultry venture or side-line.

The first consideration is the proper location of the various buildings with reference to accessibility from the house, in order to reduce the steps necessary in caring for the flock. This is an important item, far more important than the average person stops to consider. A few extra steps several times a day will amount to several extra miles in the course of a month and a good many miles in the course of a year. Besides, it consumes time, makes the poultry work a burden and, generally, might be eliminated entirely by wise planning in the beginning.

Speaking generally, the poultry buildings should be in the general direction of the other farm buildings. Many people place them in an isolated position in the opposite direction from the other farm buildings. This increases the steps and the labor necessary in handling the flock, as the feed required will have to be carried or hauled an additional distance from the cribs or bins.

If brooder houses are to be constructed, they should be planned to be the nearest to the residence of the other poultry buildings. Many people build the laying house first and later when they come, to build the brooder house have to place it farther away from the residence because the laying house was placed near the residence. This is a mistake, from an efficiency standpoint. The brooder house will require more frequent visits from the caretaker than the laying house and it should be nearest the residence.

Colony coops should be built on runners. This will, in the end provide for a considerable saving in the costs of handling the growing stock. Colony houses built on runners are practically self-cleaning, as they are simply moved to a new location by hitching a team to the runners, leaving the droppings behind. Some of these will doubtless be used for brooding baby chicks and they should be planned with substantial floors. These can, during the winter, be used for surplus laying stock, or to house the breeding pens, which are best kept separate from the general laying flock.

Another great labor-saving aid which should be utilized to the fullest advantage is the hopper system of feeding. No busy farmer can expect to attain the best results from his flock if he does not indulge in mash feeding, and this will require hoppers, and from the labor-saving standpoint, the hoppers more than justify their existence, especially in the case of growing young stock.

Fig. 6—A Farm Poultry House Built of Hollow Building Tile with Full Monitor Roof.

Where hoppers are utilized to the fullest advantage, it will be possible to handle the young stock on range with a single visit per day, largely to see that everything is all right, and, if necessary, to close the doors of the coops at night to protect the flock against enemies of field or forest. The hoppers can be built large enough so that they will require filling but once a week. This greatly reduces the overhead and labor necessary to cam' the young stock to maturity, at the season when the farmer is rushed the most by his general farm work.

Likewise, there is a great advantage in using the proper equipment to water the flock. Large founts should be purchased, founts that can be kept from freezing during winter weather. This will not only insure the maximum egg supply during cold weather, and the abundance of water has a great deal to do with it, but it will greatly lessen the labor involved

CHAPTER II

in keeping the water supply normal. Much money can be wasted in starting out by buying small and inadequate founts. Take your time, and select the best.

If you build a long, continuous laying house, make plans for a few outside doors along the center of the building. These can serve a double purpose of doors and ventilators. They will save many unnecessary steps, where it is desired to get into center pens, as one will not have to go to either end of the long building and pass through several other pens in order to reach the desired one.

In placing one-inch mesh wire over the open front openings of the pens, it will prove a great time and labor saver to place the wire on frames which are hinged and made to fit the openings. These can be opened up when it comes time to clean out the litter, and will more than pay for themselves in one season because of the labor they will save in handling the litter. A wheelbarrow or wagon box can be backed up to the window or opening and the litter forked directly into them, thus eliminating at least one extra handling. If the poultry flock is large, it will pay, if possible, to install a litter carrier on an overhead track such as is used in dairy and horse barns.

Take pains with the cement floor you lay in your houses so that they will be absolutely dry. There is one sure way to insure a dry floor and that is to use a layer of hollow tile under the cement. The dead air spaces in the tile prevent dampness coming through. We have used such floor ourself for several seasons now, through all kinds of weather, and it has never been the least bit damp. This is more of an item in the labor bill than the beginner may think, for it gets away from the almost daily changing of the litter in damp weather. And, one may rest assured, the litter has to be changed at the first sign of dampness, if the health and efficiency of the flock is to be maintained. The few extra cents spent in hollow tile will be repaid time and again in the course of the year.

As a general rule, do not plan nests under the dropping board. They are hard to get at, hard to keep clean, and provide too attractive a hiding place for lice and mites. Do not build nests or install nests that cannot be easily and quickly cleaned. This is of vast importance to the man who is producing eggs either for market or for hatching purposes, and who is not? The bottoms of the nests should be removable, as shown elsewhere in this book, so that they can be cleaned in a jiffy.

Many other labor saving devices and plans will suggest themselves to the thinking man. Use them, utilize them to the fullest advantage. They mean money in the pocket.

CHAPTER III.

The Selection of Breeds

The Meaning of Breeds— the Breeds of Economic Value to THE Farmer— How to Select the Breed to Fit THE Purpose In Mind — the Meaning of Strains and Their Value

Many people are confused as to the meaning of the term "breed." It carries a definite meaning and when incorrectly applied often causes misunderstanding. The Standard of Perfection, published by the American Poultry Association, which is the final authority on breeds and breed types for the guidance of the breeder and the judge in the show room, divides fowls into three main divisions. First, we have Classes, then Breeds and, finally. Varieties.

The term "Classes" refers to those breeds and varieties belonging to general types having points in common and classed usually according to the region in which they originated. Thus, the American Classes, Rocks, Wyandottes, Reds and Buckeyes, originated in the United States; the Mediterranean Classes, Leghorns, Anconas and Minorcas originated in Italy, Spain and the Mediterranean countries; the Asiatics, Cochins, Langshans, originated in Asiatic countries; the English Classes, Orpingtons, Dorkings, originated in England, etc. It will be noted that the term "Class" is very broad and includes a wide, general range of fowl.

The term "Breed" is narrower in its meaning, but still somewhat broader in its application than general usage among breeders and poultry raisers indicates. Generally, it applies to a race of fowls having the same general size, type and shape. The Plymouth Rock breed, for instance, applies to all fowls having the established Rock type, size and shape without reference to color markings. Thus, it may be used to mean Barred Plymouth Rocks, White, Buff or Partridge Rocks, In the case of Leghorns, it may be used to mean White, Black, Buff, Silver or Red Pyle. In Reds, it applies to either Single or Rose Comb Rhode Island Reds.

The term "Variety" is a further sub-division of the term "Breed." It means a certain definite type of fowl coming under the general breed classification. Generally, the name of the variety is taken from its most noticeable external characteristic, namely, color marking. Thus, Barred Plymouth Rocks, are a variety of the Plymouth Rock breed. White Leghorns are a variety of the Leghorn breed, and we have a further subdivision here of Rose and Single Comb. It is improper to call a variety a breed, in the larger sense and, likewise, a breed is not a variety, except in one or two isolated cases.

The Breeds of Economic Value to the Farmer

There is a multitude of breeds and varieties of chickens. Many exist merely because of their unusual color markings or extraordinary types. They have little or no economic importance, being bred chiefly as a past time and to amuse the fanciers of the ultra fancy persuasion.

Fig. 7—*Single Comb White Leghorn Hen.*

For all practical importance, the choice, or the interest of the farmer will be confined to a very few general breeds arid varieties under them because only a few have been bred to a high state of productivity and are of economic importance.

Leaving sentiment out of consideration and speaking from the standpoint of ultimate profit, the farmer will be limited in his selection at the present time to the following breeds: Rocks, Wyandottes, Reds, Brahmas, Leghorns or Minorcas. He may want to include

CHAPTER III.   25

the Orpingtons and perhaps he should, but please keep in mind that this discussion is limited to the economic side of the question; namely, the value of the breed for either meat or eggs. There are many reasons why the English fowl with their white skinned characteristics are not in favor for commercial purposes. The English fowl are not any better layers than our American classes, although they are often just as good. From a fancier's standpoint, the Orpington possesses marked advantages, but we incline to the belief that the farmer will not find it as desirable, everything considered, as the breeds mentioned.

These breeds may be further classified according to the chief purpose which they have been bred to serve. The Rocks, Wyandottes and Reds may be designated as General Purpose Fowl, because they have been developed with the double purpose in mind of securing good layers and a good market fowl. In other words, they have size. The Brahma is the sole representative of the Meat breeds which is now bred to any extent in this country. The Cochin has practically passed out. The Brahma is still the favorite for soft roasters and gives some wonderful results when crossed with White Rocks for this purpose. It may generally be ruled out of consideration, however, for the average farmer is not in a position to produce fowls for market at a profit. The average farmer must have eggs in order to secure the maximum profit.

Fig. 8—*White Wyandotte Hen, Representative of a Splendid Breed.*

The Leghorns and the Minorcas belong to the Egg breeds, their chief purpose being the production of eggs. This does not mean that they are worthless as market fowl, as so many people claim. The Minorcas compares favorably in size with many of the General Purpose breeds, and many strains of the Leghorns are bred over-size and practically as large as the Rocks or I Reds. Because of their rapid rate of development. broilers can be grown from Leghorn stock to practically the same weight in the same time as from the General Purpose breeds. This means that Leghorn surplus cockerels can be marketed early in the spring to the same advantage as any other breeds.

The farmer, if a profit is to be won from the poultry work, must make his choice from these breeds. They are the breeds which have received the most attention from the breeders and have been developed with certain purposes in mind, all of which are grounded in some economic advantage. The man who takes up another breed is merely depriving himself of the advantages offered by breed progress.

How TO Select the Breed to Fit the Purpose in Mind

It should not be a hard matter to select the breed to keep, if sentiment and mere fancy is left out of consideration. Every farmer will have a definite purpose in mind before taking up poultry work seriously. The man who takes up poultry breeding as a side-line will, in the majority of cases, desire eggs for market before all else. The man who wishes to devote his entire attention to poultry breeding may have other goals in mind, such as the production of fancy stock for the show room.

Fig. 9—*Single Comb Rhode Island Red Hen*

Whatever the purpose, each man can ascertain it by asking himself what the chief motive in his mind is. Perhaps he will want to run a hatchery. Then he will have to determine the most popular breeds and cater to the popular demand. And in the end, that popular demand is influenced by the same factors which would influence him if he were going directly into the poultry business himself. It is, in the final analysis, from the economic standpoint, either market eggs or market poultry. Where flocks are maintained merely for home use, or largely for that purpose, then other considerations will enter in.

Poultry breeds have been developed with definite purposes in mind. One race of breeders have sought egg yield more than they have sought

CHAPTER III.

anything else and they have brought down to us the egg breeds. Another class of breeders have been looking for a market fowl and have bred such fowls and have given us the Brahmas and the other fowls belonging to the meat breeds. Still another class have sought to produce a fowl of good size, that would make a good market fowl and, at the same time, lay a large number of eggs. And so we have the general or dual purpose of breeds. All the farmer has to do is to determine first what object he has in wanting to breed poultry, and then make his selection in the proper breed. He cannot go far wrong.

Fig. 10—*Columbian Plymouth Rock Hen.*

There is no such thing as the "best" breed of poultry. There are a number of "best" breeds and we feel that we have covered the outstanding ones in our recommendations above. The final choice must depend upon individual desire. There are some considerations, however, which must be taken into account and one should not allow prejudices to influence him adversely in meeting these considerations.

If eggs are to be the principal object in your poultry work, do not make the mistake of keeping any but an egg breed. Commercial poultrymen have tried time and again to make a "go" of it at egg farming with flocks of dual purpose fowls and have not succeeded, except in cases where exceptional conditions favored them. From a strict profit standpoint there can be no doubt but that the Single Comb White Leghorn is the most efficient fowl of all, but we are not always looking for the maximum profit. We do not make this statement because of individual prejudice or favoritism, but upon the authority of various experiment station investigations.

For instance, in point of feed consumed, it was found at the New Jersey Egg-laying Contests that the amount of feed consumed by heavy laying hens per year according to breed was as follows:

Leghorns	76 pounds
Wyandottes	80 pounds
R. I. Reds	87 pounds
Plymouth Rocks	90 pounds

The United States Government Poultry Farm at Beltsville, Md., has carried on some experiments along the same line, but has gone a step further and tabulated some figures to show how much feed each breed requires in order to produce one dozen eggs:

Leghorns	4.8 pounds
Leghorn yearlings	5.5 pounds
Dual purpose	6.7 pounds
Dual purpose yearlings	9.6 pounds

Other figures might be cited along similar lines, but these are sufficient to show that the Leghorn hen or pullet is the most efficient egg producer that has yet come under the eye of the investigators. An additional point to be considered is the fact that a lower housing cost per bird is required with the egg breeds than with the larger fowl, as they do not require as much floor or ground space as the larger fowls. Roughly speaking, dual purpose fowls require one-third more floor space in buildings, at least, than the egg breeds, and the meat breeds, such as Brahmas and Langshans require even more room. This will amount to a considerable item in overhead cost on a place where large flocks are to be maintained.

The Leghorns have had it pretty much their own way at the egg-laying contests so long that there is no disputing the statement that they are the most outstanding egg-laying breed now known to man. But large individual records have also been made by Rhode Island Reds in official contests, and by Rocks and Wyandottes in lesser degree. The first outstanding layer developed by an egg-laying contest was Lady Show-You, a White Plymouth Rock. Her record was more than 260 eggs.

CHAPTER III.

Fig. 11—Barred Plymouth Rock Pullet.

The most outstanding development in the breeding of high record layers has been, however, among the White Leghorns, probably due to the fact that this breed has more universally engaged the attention of the commercial poultrymen than any other. There are dozens and dozens of Leghorns having egg records over 200 eggs each in one year now in the country, and several breeders have pullet records running over 300 eggs. One breeder on the Pacific Coast, for instance, has made a tremendous development along this line and has close to three dozen such layers to his credit.

Many farmers are prejudiced against Leghorns, looking upon them as an unsatisfactory fowl for general farm purposes. We are not presenting a brief for any particular breed, as it is of slight consequence to us as to the breed selected, but we do feel the responsibility of presenting the facts. Each man can then judge for himself.

The dual purpose fowls are, in many respects, wonderful birds. Personally, we have always had more than passing interest in the Rhode Island Reds and the Plymouth Rocks. We have compared them side by side and have found them to be wonderful fowls in every respect. The Rhode Island Reds are generally great layers and, if there is any choice, are probably better layers than any of the other general or dual purpose fowl. There are, however, one or two strains of Barred Plymouth Rocks which will hold their own as layers with any other breed, the Leghorns alone excepted. One or two strains of Wyandottes have also been bred up to good egg yields, but just now we are not discussing strains but breeds in their entirety.

The Meaning of Strains and Their Value

The strain is vastly more important than the breed or variety. One flock of fowls may make a poor record during the year and another flock of the same variety and breed on a neighboring farm may earn a substantial profit. The difference is likely to be in the strain, other things being equal.

There is confusion in the minds even of certain poultry breeders as to the meaning of the term "strain", judging from their advertising matter. A strain is a certain definite family of fowls within a given variety and breed, so bred that the family characteristics have been sufficiently established along a definite line to give them a distinction over ordinary fowls in the same variety and breed. A strain is not a variety of fowls, and the fact that a man breeds a strain does not make it necessary that he should have originated his family himself. But the right to claim one's own strain is loosely used at the present time by thousands of breeders.

We have already pointed out that there is no such thing as the one "best" breed or variety of chickens; that strain is what counts for the most in this respect. By that we mean that there are certain breeders in almost every variety and breed who have, through long patience and effort, succeeded in breeding up families of fowls within their varieties and breeds that are outstanding in utility performance or show room quality, as the case may be. One can find strains in almost any breed or variety that will pay a good profit under careful handling, while other apparently well-bred fowls in the same breed or variety are practically worthless for any purpose. The difference lies in the breeding, in the inherited characteristics, in the family or strain blood.

There are, of course, certain breeds in which more strains have been developed than in other breeds and varieties; and the more strains there are developed along some definite line, the more the influence will be felt on the entire breed and variety the country over. The result will be to elevate the standard of the entire breed and variety. That is one of the reasons why Single Comb White Leghorns are so popular in the country for commercial egg farming; more strains for high egg-laying ability have been developed in this variety the past 20 years than in any other.

Many people make the common mistake of thinking that if one flock of hens in a given variety make good records that it is the breed or "kind" that counts and that any fowls masquerading under that same

CHAPTER III.

breed or variety name will be good layers. That is why so many people are constantly changing "kinds." They do not take into consideration the value of strain; they look more at the feathers, in their search for the same "kind."

It will not require a great deal of study, even for the novice, to soon learn what the best strains are in the variety he selects. An examination of the advertising pages of any good poultry journal will soon give a cross-section of the best breeders in each variety. Any editor will be glad to advise you, if you are in doubt. But do not make the mistake so many people do of buying into a strain second or third hand. This always is unsatisfactory. It pays to go to headquarters and pay the price. To buy second or third hand is to acquire all of the faults in management and care that the other fellow has foisted upon the good strain, in the majority of cases.

CHAPTER IV

Buildings and Equipment for the Flocks

Iowa Semi-Monitor House— Missouri Fool-Proof House— The Minnesota Type House— The Lord Farms Small Flock House— Colony Houses, Brooding Houses and Coops— Nests, Hoppers and Appliances

The first use of the Iowa Semi-Monitor Poultry House is generally credited to Charles Laros, an Iowa commercial poultryman living in Poweshiek county. Mr. Laros practices intensive poultry culture, carrying

Fig. 12—Iowa Semi-Monitor Type Laying House Accommodating 1,000 Layers.

larger flocks to the acre than the average farmer will find practicable, but his problems of housing were essentially the same as those confronting the farmer. He found that it was hard to secure proper ventilation from his shed roof type laying houses without also having drafty pens. The result of his experiments in this direction was the first Iowa Semi-Monitor House. It later came to the attention of the extension department of Iowa State College and was advocated widely as the most desirable farm flock house.

There was nothing essentially new in the design as the half-monitor type of construction had been advocated by Dr. P. T. Woods some 10 or 12 years before, and had been used by other authorities with variations in the intervening period.

The distinctive feature of the Iowa Semi-Monitor House is the fact that it secures proper ventilation for the laying flock in all seasons and eliminates the ills attending stuffy, damp and impure air. Many people have objected to the semi-monitor house because it was more expensive in initial cost to build. The outlay of a few extra dollars should not be questioned when such additional outlay removes one of the most serious obstacles to proper poultry housing. No doubt other forms of construc-

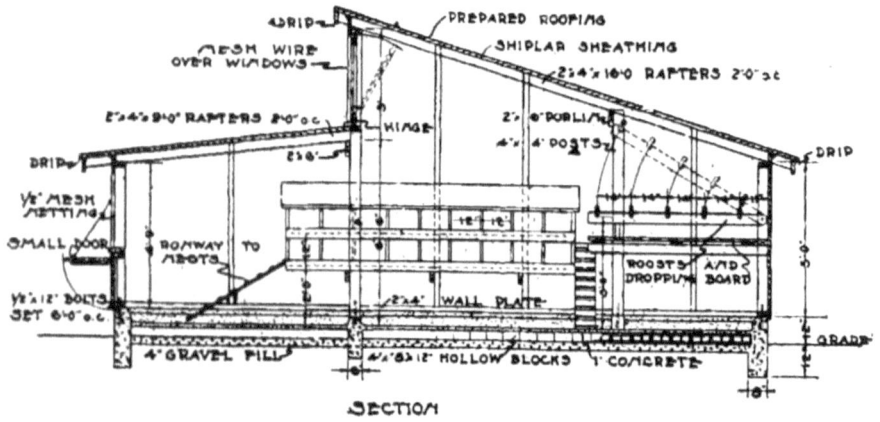

Fig. 13—Cross-section of Iowa Semi-Monitor House.

tion will secure practically the same results in ventilation at less cost, but we do not know of a laying house now in use that secures all of the advantages of the Iowa Semi-Monitor Poultry House that can be constructed for the same money.

The semi-monitor poultry house, as in the case of hog houses, makes it possible for the sunlight to reach all parts of the interior of the house during the daytime. Sunshine is the best germicide in the world, and this value should not be overlooked. Shed roof houses may be constructed to secure practically the same advantage in ventilation, but they cannot be built as wide as the semi-monitor house and also secure a flood of sunlight in the rear corners. Consequently, the shed-roof type house can seldom be built over 16 feet wide and secure sunlight on the droppings board, without running them up too high in front. This is, in itself, a waste in money and tends to make the houses excessively cold in bad weather.

The Iowa Semi-Monitor Poultry House is built in units 22 feet wide by 24 feet long. Mr. D. E. Carlson, an Iowa farmer mentioned in a preceding chapter, uses this house on his farm for his side-line flock and he has made the house 24 feet wide and considers that it is an improvement over the original plan. We are inclined to agree with him.

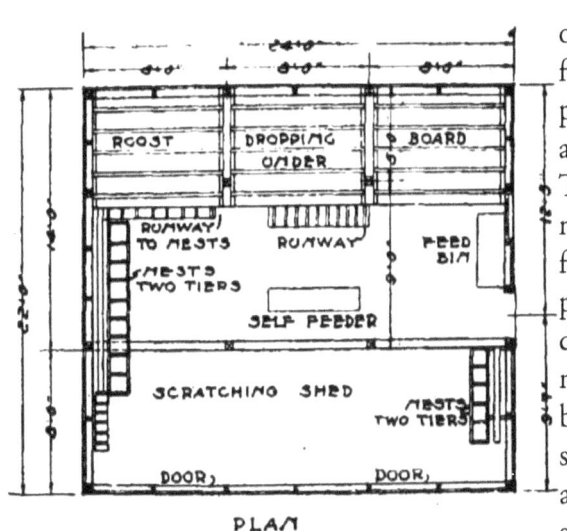

Fig. 14—Floor Plan of one unit of Pen. Iowa Semi-Monitor House.

Allowing three and one-half square feet of floor space to each hen, a pen 22x24 feet in size will accomodate 150 layers. The same house will accomodate 250 Leghorns, affording two square feet per layer as many breeders do and speaking in round numbers. The house is built in long, continuous style where larger flocks are desired, saving in construction costs and bringing the flock all under one roof. Mr. D, E. Carlson has two of these houses, one, 24x96 feet in length and another, 24x127 feet in length. The plans given will be found to be self-explanatory.

This house can be used for poultry of practically all ages and for all purposes. Muslin curtains can be placed in the shed or open front part and baby chicks brooded there with colony hovers or brooders, or the laying hens can be placed in this part of the house and the chicks given the rear and more protected portion, or one or two pens may be given over entirely to chicks until they are old enough to go to range.

Missouri Fool-Proof House

The Missouri Fool-Proof House was given to the poultry world by Prof. T. E. Quisenberry and was the result of his work at the Missouri Poultry Experiment Station at Mountain Grove. The term "fool-proof" is applied to this house because the ventilating device cannot be tampered

Fig. 15—A Row of Missouri Fool-Proof Poultry Houses.

with, is built right into the wall structure and works constantly in all kinds of weather. It has the advantage of the open-front house and, at the same time, gets away from the soiling of the litter in the interior of the house so common when sudden storms come up. The chief feature of the house is the shutter ventilator which is made of 6-inch strips set on an incline, so as to admit a free passage of air but to prevent rain or snow beating into the interior of the house and damaging the litter. This feature eliminates the disagreeable task of getting up in the middle of the night to let down muslin or burlap curtains over open front openings to protect litter and the interior of the house, in the event of a storm.

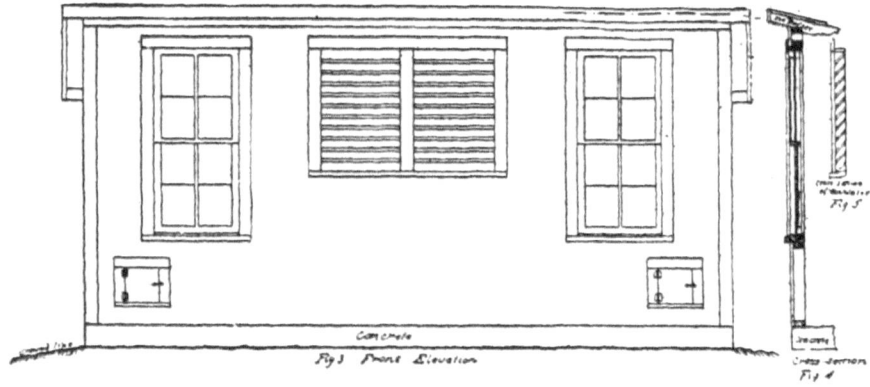

Fig. 16—Front Elevation, Missouri Fool-Proof House; also detail of Shutter Construction.

The Fool-Proof House is constructed on the shed-roof style and the most efficient size house of this type is one 16 feet wide. It should not be less than this, if maximum comfort is to be secured roosting fowls at night and it cannot be greater unless extra roof studding is used. Some farmer have constructed them 20 feet wide with good results, but they cannot be wider. They are built in the long, continuous style depending upon the number of fowls to be accommodated. The unit is a pen 20 feet long and 16 feet to 20 feet deep. One pen 20x20 will accomodate about 200 Leghorns and a less number of fowls of larger breeds.

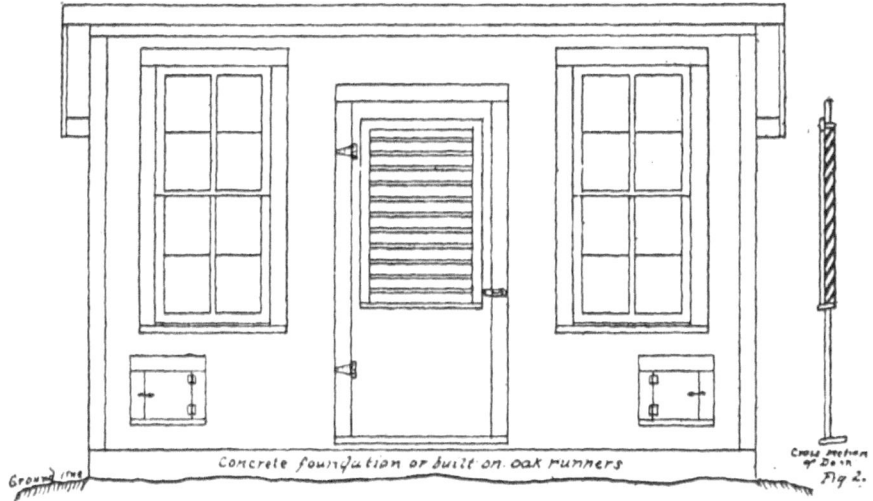

Fig. 17—Fool-Proof Shutter Adapted to Colony Coop.

When built as large laying houses in sections 20x20 feet they should be about 9 feet high in front and 5 1/2 feet high in the rear. Where built in shorter widths, as 16 feet for instance, the front can be made 8 feet high and 5 1/2 feet high at the rear.

The fool-proof method of ventilation can be adapted to any shed-roof type house with good results. It is equally serviceable in colony houses and small laying flock houses. In fact, it can be used on practically any style of poultry house to good advantage.

The fool-proof ventilating device should appeal to any busy farmer because it answers the ventilation problem and removes much of the labor necessary under other forms of construction, particularly the open-front house. It has the advantage of requiring no extra attention, and this is something every busy man will appreciate.

The Minnesota Type House

The Minnesota Type House is an adaptation of the shed-roof type house to the more severe climate of northern winters. This house is recommended for all localities where any amount of zero weather is experienced. It is absolutely frost-proof, if constructed according to the plans given and will keep a flock of laying hens in excellent condition and health, regardless of the severity of the climate.

We first ran across this type of house on the farm of Hugo Anderson, a poultryman mentioned in a preceding chapter. Mr. Anderson's farm is located within a short distance of Duluth, Minnesota, where the winters are generally very severe. In fact, Mr. Anderson stated to us that it was not uncommon for the temperature to go down to 40 degrees below zero and stay there six weeks at a time.

We visited Mr. Anderson's farm the first of December and saw yearling hens and cock birds which had been carried through the previous severe winter without a single frost-bitten comb! It seemed incredible and we dropped the remark that the cocks looked like cockerels and the hens like pullets. It seemed impossible that there should not be a frosted comb in the lot. Mr. Anderson asked us to examine the spurs on the male birds and we saw that they were, indeed, yearlings.

"You want to know why we don't have frosted combs up here?" he asked. "Well, that is due entirely to the method we use in the construction of our laying houses.

"The front walls of the houses, which face the south, have two thicknesses of boards, between which there is a layer of heavy building paper. The other three walls have this outside double thickness, then there is an inside wall of matched lumber which creates a dead-air space in between, in addition. The most important detail is found, however, in the construction we use in our roofs. Oftentimes, you know, people take great pains with their side walls and then forget all about the possibility of frost entering the house through the roof. There is also a double wall with a dead-air space between in the roof construction, the under wall of matched lumber being nailed on first. Then the space normally devoted to a dead-air section is filled up tight with sawdust and the top side of the roof is put in place and roofing paper over it. This gives us a roof construction through which frost never enters, and that is the big reason why we haven't any frosted combs on our place. It gets cold enough up here for that, all right!

"As for ventilation, I have found that the best plan for our northern winters is to have large, full-length windows in every pen and to keep these windows closed tight during cold weather. Fresh air is supplied through a ventilator at the top of each window, which is just the width of

Fig. 18—An Adaptation of the Minnesota Laying House, as used on Oak Dale Farms.

the windows and 18 inches high. There is one of these for each window. This ventilator is merely a muslin-covered frame, hinged at the bottom and which opens inward at the top, throwing the incoming air against the roof and preventing it sweeping down upon the backs of the hens. This supplies sufficient fresh air, and is the plan recommended by the Minnesota station for this climate. In storming weather the frame is closed to keep rain and snow out, and yet sufficient air penetrates the muslin to keep the stock in excellent condition."

Mr. Anderson's contention that this house kept the stock in excellent condition in his climate was verified by the writer, who had ample evidence before his eyes in the large flock of yearlings shown him by Mr. Anderson. They were in the pink of condition, in such excellent color and vigor that one could hardly believe that they were not pullets just in off the range. The fact that these yearlings made a 40 per cent egg record the day we visited the farm, December 1, also indicates something.

The Lord Farms Small Flock House

The accompanying plans illustrate a laying house that is particularly well adapted to general farm usage. It was perfected by Lord Farms, a large commercial egg plant, which has specialized in market eggs for 20

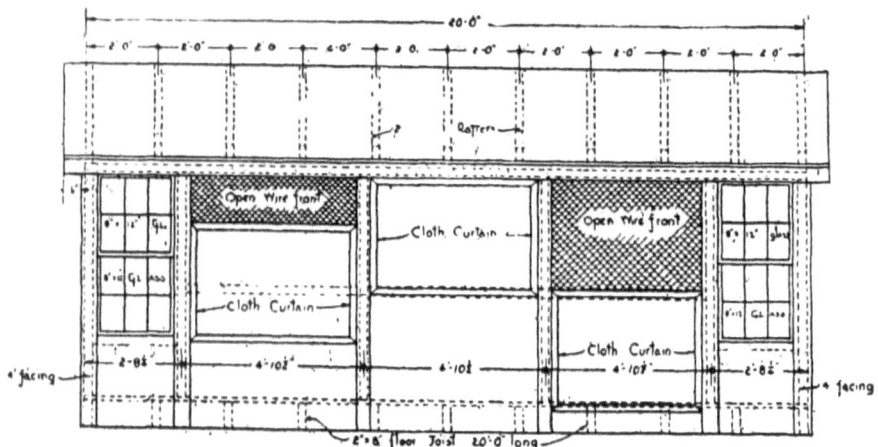

Fig. 19—Front Elevation Lord Farms Small Flock Laying House For 150 to 200 Layers.

years and which has tried and tested almost every kind of a house known. This house is based upon the Cornell poultry house and is practically identical with that house, except for a few improvements which lessen the labor involved in regulating the curtains, and which provides more openings on the front.

It is significant to note that many of the larger commercial breeders are getting away from the large flock unit houses and are going back to smaller flocks and building their houses accordingly. They have come to the conclusion, and it is a very pertinent one, that small flocks make better flock records than large flocks, under average conditions.

This house has been adopted by the Lord Farms and other breeders as giving the very best flock results, and being the most economical to construct. It is safe to say that no farmer can get along with a house smaller than the one shown herewith, if he raises any poultry at all.

A house 20x20 feet, as the one here shown, will accomodate all the way from 150 to 200 Leghorns, and a smaller number of larger fowls. It offers the advantage of calling for a small initial outlay of cash in buildings and making it possible to expand as the flock grows.

CHAPTER IV

In these plans we have a good example of the proper pitch to place on a double pitch roof for the best results. The double-pitched roof is especially valuable on a wide building. A house with a low wall behind, and a shed roof construction, is very hard to clean because the attendant has to stoop over in order to get at the dropping boards, but a double-pitch roof on the same building will add convenience in doing this work. Double-pitched roofs are also cooler in summer and warmer' in winter than the shed-roof type, if not built too high in front and at too great a pitch, provided there is an outlet for the warm air, as indicated in the plans for this building.

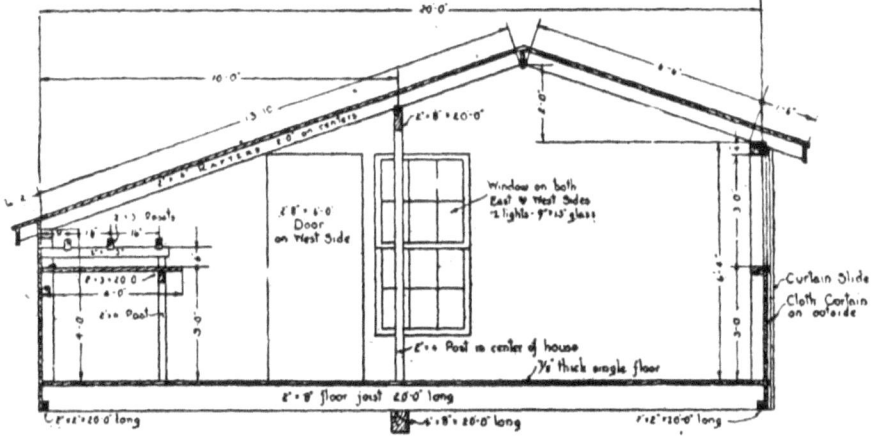

Fig. 20—Cross-section Lord Farms Small Flock Laying House.

This house is not too large to be constructed upon runners or skids so that it can be moved from place to place and used as a colony coop for the growing stock, if deemed advisable, or it can be constructed upon a permanent foundation.

One feature worthy of special mention is the system of ventilation. It will be noticed that there are three sliding muslin frames on the front of the building. These are for the purpose of covering the open windows in stormy weather so that rains and snow cannot beat in and soil the litter, or for cold nights when it is desired to give the hens additional protection. Most of these muslin frames on the average house are either hinged on the outside or inside of the openings. If on the outside, the wind soon destroys them, while if on the inside they soon become dust-filled and dirty and do not do full duty in ventilating the interior, necessitating the changing of the cloth continually. By placing them on frames in grooves on the front of the building as shown in this plan, they are always in position for use and can be adjusted to any height deemed necessary, something that is impossible in the case of hinged frames, which are usually either entirely open or entirely closed. Likewise, it is not necessary for the attendant to enter the house in order to adjust the frames. All this work can be done from the outside in a few second's time.

The house is planned to face the south and there are windows on both the east and the west sides of the building, another advantage for summer ventilation that is too often overlooked on the average farm poultry house, and entirely impossible in the long, continuous style of poultry house. The two windows on the front provide ample light on dark days when the muslin frames have to be entirely closed.

Colony Houses, Brooding Houses and Coops

Colony houses and coops are necessary where a large number of young chicks are to be matured. These houses are not necessarily of expensive cost in construction. They should be built upon runners or skids in order to make them portable, unless a permanent location is chosen

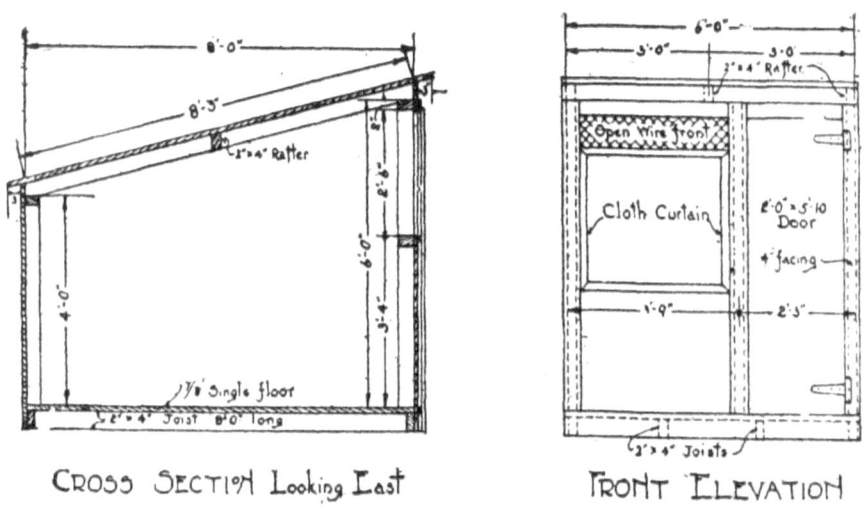

Fig. 21—Colony Coop for 100 Baby Chicks.

for them in ideal surroundings, as in an orchard. Colony houses make it possible to establish a unit in flock size in which to mature young stock, and as the number matured increases each year to add to the number of

CHAPTER IV

coops. Where the coops are properly built and of the best size, they can be used during the rest of the year for surplus laying stock or cockerels.

Colony Brooder Coop for 100 Chicks

The accompanying plans show a simple form of construction for a colony coop 6x8 feet in size, sufficient for raising 100 chicks with an oil burning brooder on range. The coop is 4 feet high in the rear, 6 feet high

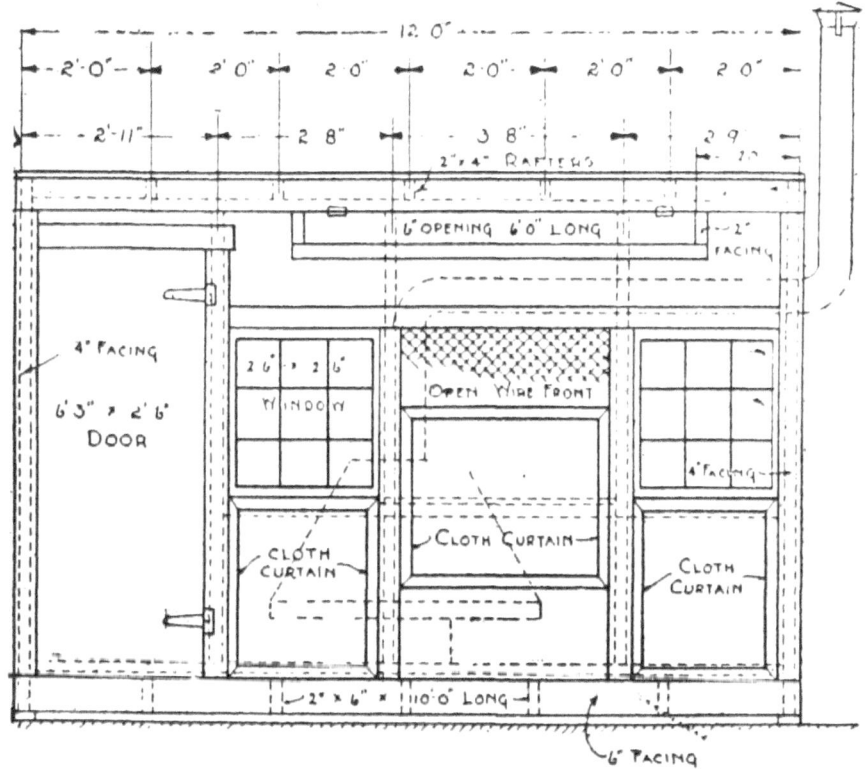

Fig. 22—Front Elevation Coal Burning Brooder House for Large Flock of Chicks.

in front, and may, or may not, be built on runners. The front is equipped with a door permitting access to the interior, and making it possible to protect the chicks at night against natural enemies. It also has an open front window, equipped with a sliding muslin-covered wooden frame to keep out the rain or to prevent chilling of the chicks on cold days. The plans are self-explanatory.

This coop is economical in cost of construction and when properly built will last for a life-time.

Coal Burning Brooder House

This house is 10x12 feet in size and designed especially for larger flocks of chicks brooded under portable coal burning brooder stoves. It is 4 feet 8 inches high at the rear and 6 feet 8 inches high in front. A sliding window is placed on the east side of the coop (the coops always face the south) and additional ventilation is afforded by windows and openings

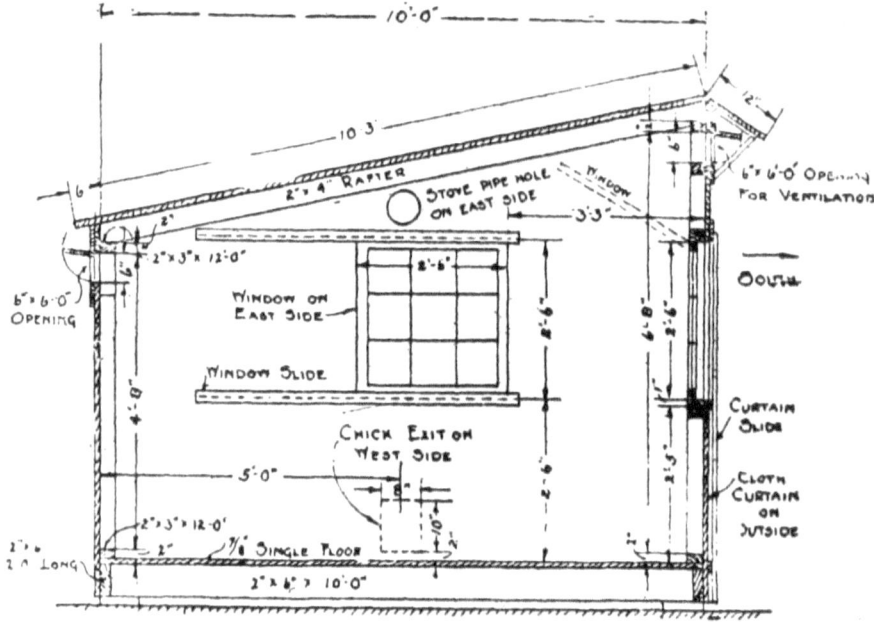

Fig. 23—Cross-section Coal Burning Brooder House.

on the south or front and an opening in the rear wall 6 inches wide by 6 feet long. A similar opening is provided in front close under the roof. These devices keep the coop cool in the hottest summer weather, something absolutely necessary to prevent over-heating, crowding, losses and stunted chicks. One common fault with many colony coops is that they do not make maximum summer ventilation possible, and probably the greatest losses in growing stock is due to this one cause. The openings are all so arranged that they can be closed when desirable, and so that the house can be properly ventilated, regardless of the direction of the wind, and the brooder stove thereby regulated so that it will not burn out, or

CHAPTER IV

suck out. The plans give full directions for construction of this type house. The portable coal burning brooder stove is placed in the exact center of the floor and it is well to make the floor double thickness immediately under it.

Semi-Monitor Colony Coops

The accompanying illustration shows the semi-monitor colony coop used by Charles Laros in his orchard on his Iowa poultry farm. It follows the semi-monitor form of construction is 10x12 feet in size and is built on a permanent foundation, although there is no reason why this coop could not be built on runners and moved from place to place. A coop of this kind is more expensive to construct than ordinary shed-roof colony coops, but it is probably more durable and can be used to better advantage the year around for laying stock or surplus breeders or cockerels.

Fig. 24—Semi-Monitor Colony Coop Used by Charles Laros.

Range Boosting Coop

Fig. 25—Range Roosting Coop.

This coop has been used with good success by a Dallas county, Iowa, poultry farmer for roosting quarters for young stock on grass range in a young orchard. It has no floor and is intended only for chicks after they have been taken from the brooder house and are able to take care of themselves on the range. It is merely a roosting shelter, has two flat perches, and is cleaned by moving to a new location. It can be built any convenient size, 4x6 feet and 6x8 feet being the most convenient sizes.

Small Flock Breeding House

Fig. 26—Small Flock Breeding Houses Used by D. E. Carlson on His Iowa Farm.

D. E. Carlson, an Iowa farmer, uses these 6x8 feet individual pens for his breeding flocks, which are isolated, as they should be, from the laying flocks and are given individual yards so that they cannot range with the other stock. There is nothing special in the arrangement of these coops. Three window sashes are placed in front, hinged at the top to open outward. This affords sufficient ventilation and protects the interior of the coops from beating storms. A small door is placed on the east side (opposite in picture) to permit access for gathering the eggs and cleaning the coop.

Two-Pen Small Flock Breeding Coop

The illustration shows a two-pen breeding flock pen which has been used for several seasons by the author. It is 10x12 feet in size, 7 feet high in front and 5 feet high at the rear. This coop will comfortably house two breeding pens

Fig. 27—Two- Pen Small Flock Breeding Coop.

of 15 females each, and a laying flock of up to 50 Leghorns can be maintained in it, by slight crowding; in fact, one winter 55 fowls were kept in this coop with good results. It was built of old lumber and shows what can sometimes be done with waste material. The only new material used was the framing and it was new only because we had no second-hand material available.

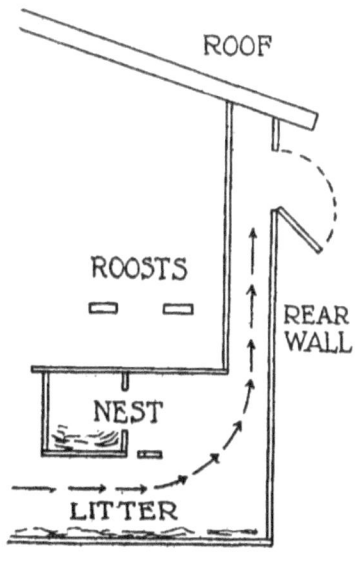

Fig. 28—Rear Wall Ventilating Device of Fig. 27.

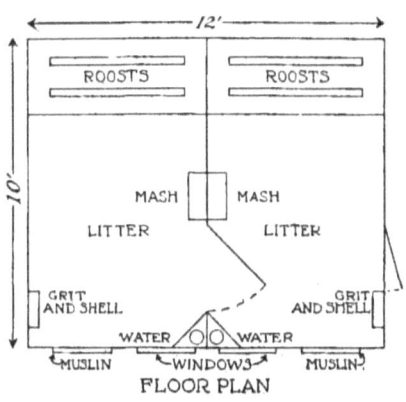

Fig. 29—Showing Interior Arrangement of Fig. 27.

A feature of this coop is the ventilation afforded by the large open windows protected by muslin covered frames opening outward and held in place by ordinary storm sash holders. The ventilation principle is fully illustrated by the accompanying drawing. Particular attention is called to the opening at the rear of the house which is so arranged that air may constantly play through the house when the fowls are on the roost without subjecting them to drafts. We have found this house exceptionally cool in summer and extremely satisfactory in winter. In severe weather, the opening at the rear is closed by hooking up the hinged cover.

Nests, Hoppers and Appliances

Properly constructed nests will lighten the labor load the farmer will be called upon to carry when he has his flock developed to its maximum size. Nests should be so constructed that the bottom can be slipped out easily, thus making cleaning practically automatic. This is one of those details which cannot well be overlooked, for it is of more importance to the busy man than one might think at first thought.

A number of plans are given herewith for various types of nests which can be used in the laying house. For general use on the farm, we advise against the construction of nests under the dropping boards, especially where the labor item is to be of some moment, because these nests

Fig. 30—One Method of Construction to Save Space on Inside of Laying House.

are generally hard to get at and keep clean, and they are very difficult to keep free from mites, once these pests get into the house.

A sufficient range of nest types are given to fit almost any preference or condition. Very good nests can also be purchased upon the open market, if one can afford to buy them. Galvanized iron nests and nesting cabinets are especially recommended because of the ease with which they can be kept free of vermin. Ordinary orange boxes make excellent nests, each box making two compartments by simply taking off half of the side, or one of the side boards. These are inexpensive and can be placed on wall shelves around the laying pens, or in tiers, one above the other.

CHAPTER IV

Trap Nests

Fig. 31—Darkened Nest Compartment for Wall Use.

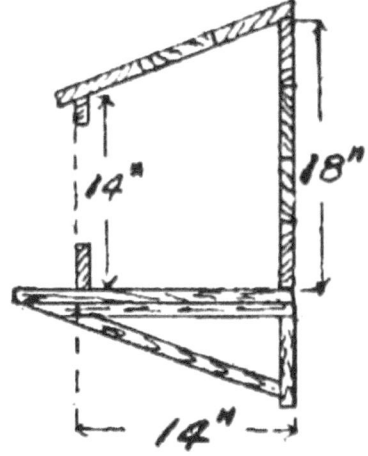

Fig. 32—Simple Wall Nest.

Trap nests are not necessary for the farm laying flock unless one desires to engage in specialty breeding for high record individuals. If pedigreeing is to be practiced, trap nests are essential and when one goes into the poultry business as a life calling, the sooner trap nesting is commenced, the better. It is the sure route to a high egg-laying strain, and it tells no lies. There is no guess-work involved. It writes the record of every hen from day to day.

Trap nests can be purchased on the open market, or they can be made right at home as preferred. Two plans are shown herewith for home-made trap nests which have proved successful. One was developed by Cornell University and the other is recommended by the Missouri Experiment Station. The plans show the dimensions and give full working details.

Hoppers and Feed Boxes

Hopper feeding of dry mashes is not only a great labor saver, if the hoppers are large enough to hold several day's supply, but is absolutely necessary if the maximum results are to be expected from the flock, regardless of age. For laying hens and growing stock, it supplies the necessary balanced ration in the unlimited quantities necessary for heavy egg yield or consistent growth and development.

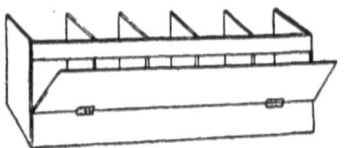

Fig. 34—Another View of Nests to Go Under Dropping Board.

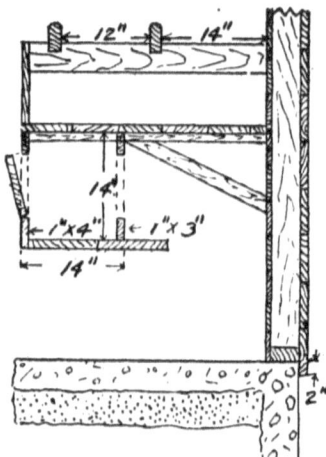

Fig. 33—For Nests Under Dropping Board (Side View).

Hoppers may be purchased on the market at a reasonable price, the majority of which are constructed of galvanized iron and will last an ordinary life-time, if given proper care. These hoppers come in many sizes and in many designs. Some are very good and some are very poor. The poultryman or farmer should make a careful examination of hoppers and select only those which will handle the mash efficiently, preventing the stock from wasting the feed. The tendency in purchasing hoppers for large flocks is to buy them too small in size to secure the maximum efficiency, so far as the labor of filling is concerned. Small hoppers have to be filled frequently, and this multiplies the labor necessary to handle the flock.

Any handy man or boy can make excellent hoppers for the flock right at home with no more complicated tools than a hammer and saw.

CHAPTER IV

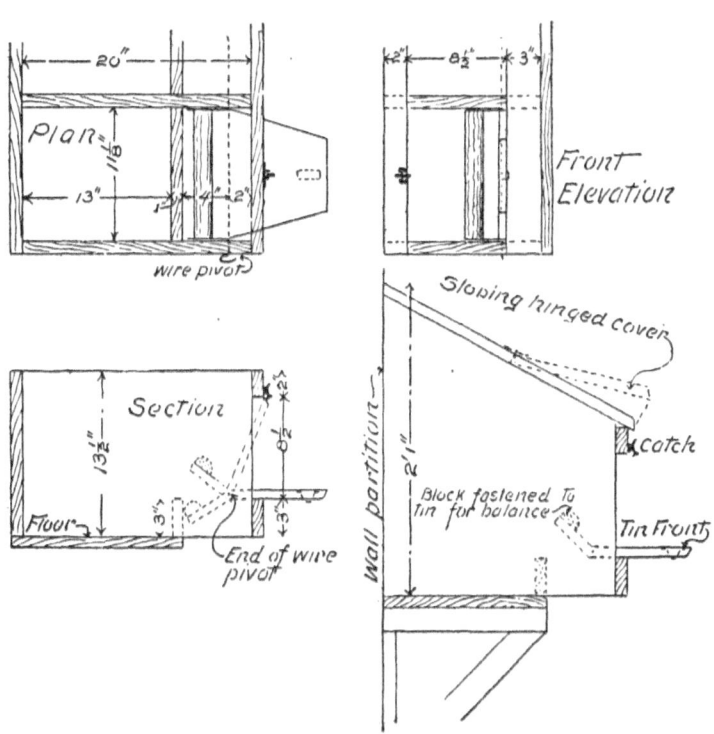

Fig. 35—Cornell Trap-Nest.

Special attention is called to the large flock hopper designed by Lord Farms. This hopper will hold sufficient dry mash for 100 birds for one week. It stands up out of the litter where straw cannot be scratched into the feeding opening, provides a pan for water, and has a revolving top to prevent fowls roosting there and soiling the mash below. One of these hoppers in the middle of each laying pen will solve the dry mash feeding problem and be the most efficient that can be secured. They can be made right on the farm on rainy days of material at hand. The plans give full details for their construction,

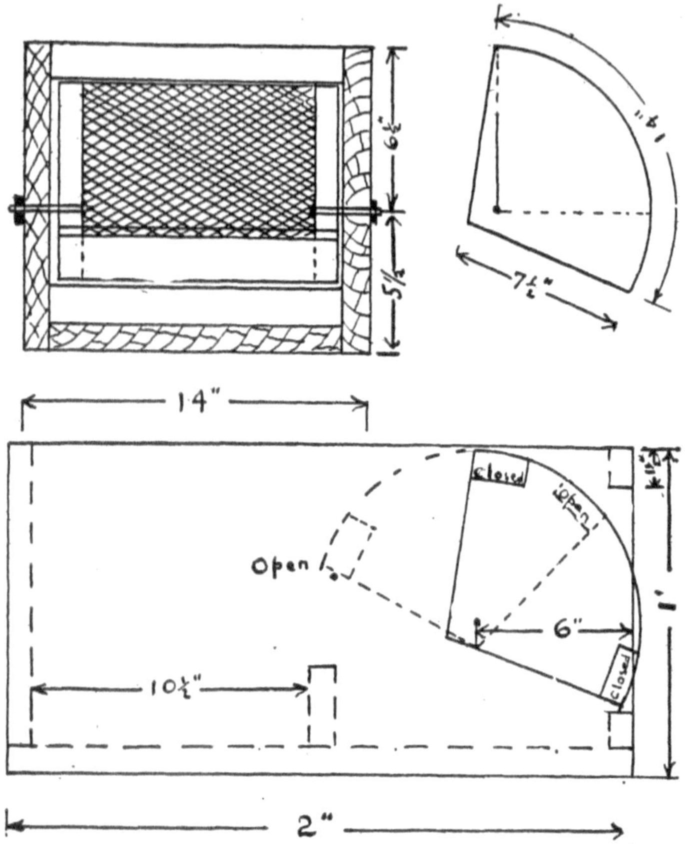

Fig. 36—Missouri Trap Nest.

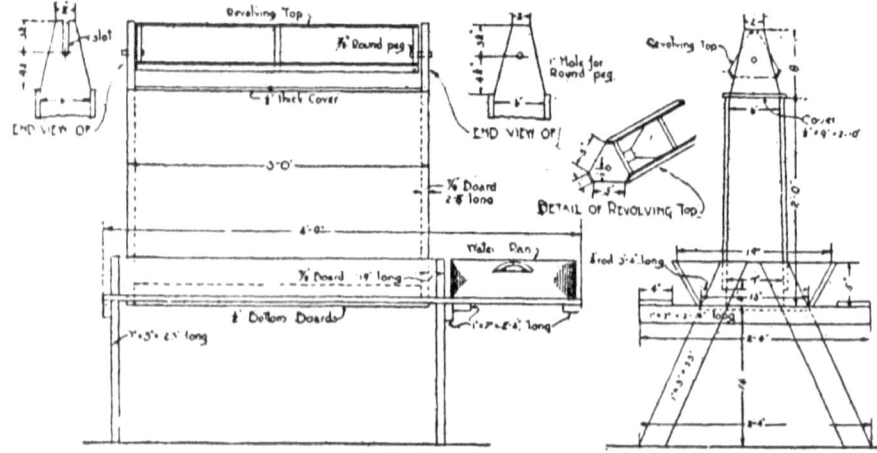

Fig. 37—Lord Farms Large Flock Hopper.

CHAPTER V

The Laws and Principles of Breeding

The Fundamental Laws of Breeding— Line Breeding— Inbreeding— Cross-Breeding— Grading— Selecting THE Breeding Stock

Fig 38.—*These Fine White Rocks Are the Result of Proper Breeding.*

When the farmer takes up the business of breeding poultry or live stock he is entering a most fascinating work. Here he comes in close contact, if he studies the forces with which he often unconsciously works, with the laws of nature, of the development of races of living things. Breeding is a science and it calls for the most painstaking study and work at the hands of the breeder. Men and women have devoted life-times to this work and have laid down the work at the end of their lives conscious of the many things yet to be learned and applied. Yet tremendous progress has been made in breeding in a single generation, especially in the poultry world.

There is one great reward in the business of the breeder and that is that it will never become standardized to the extent that feeding is, or housing. It can never be reduced to a definite formula. It must always be dependent upon the individual skill of the breeder himself. This means that the large rewards are going to flow to the man or woman who masters the science and learns how to bend it to a definite purpose or accomplishment. There are hundreds of so-called "breeders" in the poultry world today, but one could probably name the real breeders on the fingers of one hand. The same is true in the respective live stock worlds. This does not mean that only the especially fortunate can succeed at this work; it merely means that the man or woman who takes the pains to really try to understand the laws of breeding and to apply them are the ones who will reap the greatest reward. For the vast majority are content to "let Nature take its course" and to ride the crest of the waves with others who have achieved the distinction by buying into their strains. That is why success brings monetary reward to the trail blazer.

Heredity

Heredity is the very first law of breeding with which we must concern ourselves. It is the transmission of characters in the reproduction of living things. The force of the law of heredity is everywhere apparent about us. Two eggs may be absolutely identical in appearance, size, shape, color, weight. They may hatch chicks that are identical in size, shape, color, weight and appearance, but almost instantly the power of heredity asserts itself and we find one chick developing into a Barred Plymouth Rock and the other into a Silver Laced Wyandotte. Or, we may have two large white eggs which develop, respectively, into a White Leghorn fowl and a Black Minorca.

One of the first noticeable signs of the law of heredity in the actions of baby chicks is the tendency to scratch for their feed. Oftentimes baby chicks at the very first feeding on a clean board or a paper will try to scratch for their feed when there is no actual need for it. That is an evidence of the effect of heredity upon them. The fact that pullets commence to lay at a certain time is another evidence of this law.

All organisms receive directly either from single or double parent forms an inheritance of (1) racial and (2) individual characters. Racial characters take on the form of the breed and the variety to which the chick traces its ancestry, subject to certain exceptions noted later in this discussion. A racial character may be color markings, the size and shape of the comb or ear lobes, feathered or clean legs, or four or five toes, as the case may be. Individual characters, however, are not subject to such a clear classification because they are as numerous as the sands of the seashore.

While the law of heredity is apparently absolute and inflexible and one hears people talking glibly about "like begetting like" it is, nevertheless true that Nature never produces two individuals exactly alike. Pullets coming from the same parentage will vary greatly in egg production; cockerels coming from similar matings will develop into extraordinary and worthless breeding individuals; fowls from the same mating will develop combs varying in the number of points, in the color of the eyes, in color markings, in tail carriage and in innumerable other respects. This gives rise to another great law of breeding, practically as powerful as the first, which is the law of variation.

Variation

Variation appears in response to the law that no two things are reproduced exactly alike. The casual or indifferent breeder moves along the line of heredity secure in his belief that "like begets like" and content to examine no further. As a result, he makes slight progress. On the other hand, the careful and scientific breeder sees in the law of variation his great opportunity for improvement of his stock along the desired line. He is a keen judge of individuals and he is constantly weighing the individual characters of his birds or stock in an effort to improve characteristics in his individuals or breed by utilizing the law of variation.

At least one popular breed of fowls is the result of this law, worked out almost entirely by Nature. Now and then an apparently "regular" mating will produce an individual or individuals having marked characteristics differing from those of the immediate ancestry. These individuals are called "sports." White Plymouth Rocks, for instance, originated as "sports" from a mating of Barred Plymouth Rocks; the Concord grape is a sport of the native wild grape, and Moore's Early a sport of the Concord.

Pig. 39—Line-breeding Tends to Secure Uniformity in Individual Characters.

There is a marked tendency on the part of "sports" to breed true to form, hence the probable source of new breeds and types, and evidence of the desire of Nature to fortify these individuals against losing all that had been gained through disappearance of the new type. They are most noticeable where the variation is in color markings or some outward departure from general or racial characters which call attention to them, but there is no reason to assume that "sports" do not occur, in a sense, in other characters not so noticeable, such as egg laying ability.

The careful breeder is always on the alert, at any rate, to take into consideration any variation that appears and to work accordingly. But variation is not always in the direction of progress; it may be either up or down. This gives rise to another law of breeding, atavism or reversion.

Reversion

Reversion is the tendency to revert back to the type or characters of some remote or immediate ancestor. As a rule the term is applied to signify an undesirable ancestor, although the law often works to an advantage, as in the case of line-breeding where the offspring are more likely to revert back to the type and characters of a desirable and outstanding ancestor. But this only serves to emphasize the great care with which the breeder must move.

Reversion is one of the greatest stumbling blocks in the path of the breeder, particularly the line-breeder who is attempting to make progress in the type and characteristics of his strain. He cannot make this progress unless he ruthlessly eliminates every individual that is not up to the high standard set in his matings and he must constantly improve that standard by -selecting the best individuals possible with each mating, or the tendency to revert back to the undesirable ancestor crops out to bring his work to naught.

Prepotency

One hears a great deal about prepotency, especially in regard to sires used in breeding for heavy egg production; in fact, the word has come to be applied in utility breeding almost exclusively to that thought. Prepotent fowls are those especially strong in some desirable characteristic; that is, the characteristic is so firmly stamped in their blood that it is bound to be transmitted by them to their progeny.

Where careful and patient selection of breeding birds is practiced through several generations, having in mind constantly some desirable characteristic or ideal to which the breeder wishes to bring his flock, the fusion of these qualities is going, at some time, to cause progress in the direction desired to take place. By a constant selection and mating of birds in this direction, the time will come when the quality will be so firmly established in the blood lines that it becomes a distinguishing feature of the strain. This will result in the production of birds which not only possess the characteristic but also have the power to transmit it in increased measure to their progeny or offspring. These birds are prepotent, and are to be highly valued for breeding purposes.

Breeders often work for several years before they secure prepotent individuals of the type or characteristic desired in order to use them as the foundation for their real breeding operations. Iii the case of egg production, a prepotent male generally comes from a long line of good laying - dams and he may have heavy-laying grandams on the sire side in addition. It is fairly well established now that the transmission of the egg-laying ability runs from dam to son and from son to daughter, although there is some evidence to give credence to the view that it may go down from dam to daughter and daughter to daughter, as well. A prepotent sire having such a record behind him is of almost priceless value to the breeder, and the constant search of every breeder is for indications of prepotency.

The trap-nest and pedigree breeding is the only way in which they can be discovered, once produced. Likewise, it is necessary to retain the breeding birds until the performance of their progeny has been checked up to know, oftentimes, that we have such a bird among the breeders. After a time, however, the intensification of the blood lines along the desired characteristic will reach such a point that it can be said, for practical purposes, that the birds are all prepotent.

Line-Breeding

We now come to a consideration of a system of breeding which seems to be very slightly understood by the rank and file of the breeders the country over. Two thirds of the questions that are asked by those engaged in poultry breeding work is: "Just what is line-breeding? How can it be distinguished from inbreeding?"

Stated in the plainest possible language line-breeding is scientific or systematic inbreeding. This calls for an explanation of inbreeding, which we have reserved for consideration in a succeeding paragraph.

We have already pointed out that every individual bird possesses a number of characteristics distinguishing it from every other bird. Let us suppose that a breeder possesses an exceptional bird in which the characteristics are extremely desirable. Such a bird is met with so rarely that the chance of producing another like it is extremely remote. The breeder naturally desires to preserve the desirable characteristics of this bird. How can he do it?

If he merely crosses it with another bird, he cannot hope to save the characteristic because every time the progeny is crossed with another bird of the same generation, a number of other variations will be introduced into the blood which overcome the desirable ones. The result is, through mating with unrelated stock the blood of the desirable specimen is gradually bred out and lost. Obviously, the breeder cannot adopt that plan, if he is to make progress.

The result is that he must resort to line-breeding in order, not only to hold the desirable characteristic but to strengthen and preserve it in the progeny. What does he do? He looks around for the most desirable bird of the opposite sex that he can find in his yards, because he wants to stay within the family or general blood running through his fowls; the chances of unknown variations cropping out in the progeny are lessened thereby. He selects a bird that will tend, by its own characteristics to strengthen those wherein the first bird is weak. He mates them together and the result of such a mating will be to produce progeny as good or a little better than the parents.

Both males and females are secured as a result of this first mating. If the breeder is to make progress, he must intensify the blood of the original desirable specimen, for in the first generation of progeny he has only 50 per cent of it, the other 50 per cent coming from the other bird in the original mating. Let us suppose that the original male is the desirable specimen. The breeder then selects the best daughter of this male and mates her back to her father. This gives him a generation containing 75 per cent of the blood of the original sire and only 25 per cent of the original dam. He then selects the best grand-daughter, the result of this mating, and mates her back to her grandfather, the original male. This gives him a generation containing seven eighths of the blood of the original sire and only one eighth the blood of the original dam. If the original sire is still suitable for breeding, he is mated to the best female resulting, and the progeny of this mating will contain thirteen-sixteenths the blood of the original sire. It will be noted that something is gained every mating in the direction of intensifying the desirable blood. But we still cannot hold it without resorting to close inbreeding. So we develop a female line out of the original dam by the very same process, in order that we may create a female line carrying practically the full blood of the original dam. The result is that two lines are established in which the blood of the original sire predominates in one, and the blood of the original dam in the other.

By going a step farther and taking two birds of the same generation to breed together, one from the sire line and another from the dam line, a third line can be established carrying equal parts of the blood of the original birds, and this is accomplished without breeding brothers and sisters together.

This is best illustrated by referring to the accompanying chart taken from the line-breeding system of I. K. Felch, long a prominent Light Brahma breeder and one of the founders of the American Poultry Association. The explanation of this chart as given by the late Mr. Felch follows:

"Each dotted line represents the female as having been selected from the connected upper group, while the solid line shows the male as having been taken from the indicated upper group. Each circle represents the progeny. To-wit: female No. 1 mated with male No. 2 produces group No. 3, which is one-half the blood of sire and dam.

"Females from group No. 3, mated back to their own sire No. 2, produce group No. 5, which is 3/4 the blood of the sire, No. 2, and 1/4 the blood of the dam, No. 1.

"A male from group No. 3, mated back to his own dam. No. 1, produces group No. 4, which is 3/4 the blood of the dam, No. 1, and 1/4 the blood of the sire. No. 2.

"We select a cockerel from group No. 5 and a pullet from group No. 4, or vice versa, which will produce group No. 7. This is mathematically half the blood of the original pair, No. 1 and No. 2. This is a second step towards producing a new line.

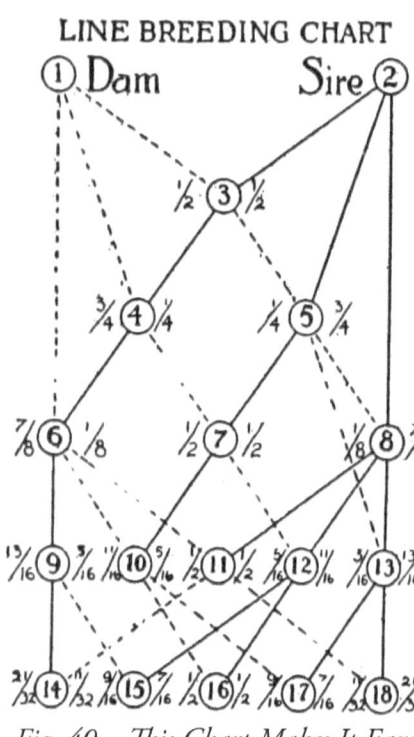

Fig. 40—*This Chart Makes It Easy to Follow Line Breeding.*

"Females from No. 5 mated back to the original male. No. 2. produce group No. 8, that are 7/8 the blood of No. 2. A cockerel from No. 4, mated back to the original dam. No. 1, produces group No. 6 that is 7/8 the blood of the original dam and only 1/8 the blood of the original sire.

"Again we select a male from No. 8 and females from No. 6 and for a third time produce chicks (in group No. 11) that are half the blood of the original pair. This is the third step and the seventh mating in securing complete breeding of our new strain. In all this we have not broken the line of sires, for every one has come from a group in which the preponderance of blood was that of the original sire. Nos. 2, 8, 13 and 18 are virtually the blood of No. 2.

"We have reached a point where we may wish to establish a male line whose blood is virtually that of our original dam, and we now select from No. 6 a male which we mate with a female from No. 4, and produce group No. 9, which is 13-16 the blood of the original dam, No. 1, and 3-16 the blood of the original sire.

"Again we select a male from No. 9 and a female of the new strain No. 11, and produce group No. 14 which becomes 21-32 of the blood of the original dam, thus preserving her strain of blood.

"A male from No. 13, which is 13-16 the blood of the original sire, No. 2, mated from females of No. 10, which are 5-16 the blood of the original sire. No. 2, gives us group No. 17, which is 9-16 the blood of

CHAPTER V

said sire, while in No. 16 we have the new strain, and in No. 18 the strain of our original sire. No. 2. Thus, we have three distinct strains, and by and with this systematic use we can go on breeding for all time to come."

Inbreeding

The breeding of fowls of close blood relationship is inbreeding. Although many people have the idea that line-breeding is apart from inbreeding and gets away from it entirely, the fact remains that line-breeding is inbreeding, but inbreeding to a purpose and of fowls more remotely related so that the evils from close inbreeding are not so likely to be apparent. But the breeder must ever keep in mind that it is inbreeding that he is practicing and that faults will be intensified as well as desirable qualities. This calls for the most persistent and painstaking selection possible of the birds used in the matings to preclude the possibility of the fault-variations over-turning or over-shadowing the desirable characteristics.

Fig. 41 —*A Desirable Type of Sire to Head the Breeding Pen.*

Close inbreeding such as brother to sister and indifferent inbreeding where no selection of individuals is made must be avoided. There is, however, no justification for the notion that all inbreeding is to be shunned and passed by, and there is ample proof that line-breeding is the only system of breeding yet devised which will enable the breeder to make any headway in his work. There is no denial of this fact; the evidence is too overwhelming.

Persistent mating of close blood relations, such as brother and sister for several generations, will unquestionably result in serious trouble. There will be a loss of size, of constitutional vigor and fecundity. On the other hand line-breeding, or systematic inbreeding, can be made to work in the opposite direction, the vigor of the stock actually increasing with each generation, the fecundity instead of being impaired, being bred up to a high point, and constitutions strengthened.

Cross-Breeding

Nothing of permanence, on the other hand, can be gained by cross-breeding or out breeding. Where birds of different varieties are mated together or birds of different strains within a variety are mated, the tendency is to destroy or break down the blood lines and cause the progeny to show variations from the types of the parent birds. First crosses often apparently show progress and indicate that something has been gained, but one cannot go back of first crosses with any degree of certainty.

There is no justification today, in the light of what we know about breeding, for anyone keeping up the practice of cross-breeding. In the matter of increased size for market poultry, it may be satisfactory where first crosses are produced to sell for market fowls, but there is no defense to the plea that it improves fecundity and makes a better race of layers. Breeders have long since found that this claim is groundless and that the tendency is, in fact, to impair and break down fecundity, if any effect is registered. First crosses often do, however, possess good fecundity but that is about as far as one can safely go. The tendency seems to ebb with each cross.

The only absolutely certain plan of breeding, one that will offer the maximum possibility of progress whatever the characteristic desired, is to keep pure-bred stock, stick to a single strain and practice line-breeding.

Grading Up the Flock

Grading is commonly practiced by live stock feeders and breeders for the purpose of improving common stock through the introduction of pure-bred sires. It has not been as commonly practiced by farmers on poultry flocks as it should be. It offers an economical way in which to improve common or mongrel stock and bring the flock to a pure-bred basis, for all practical purposes, within a few years.

The plan is to select pure-bred males or a single male and breed to the common or mongrel flock of females. All mongrel or cross-bred males are rigorously removed from the flock each season and the original males used as long as they have any breeding value. If it is necessary to secure new pure-bred males for the later crosses, they should come from the same source as the original pure-bred males and, if possible, be related to them.

The accompanying diagram illustrates the rapid progress that takes place in grading. It will be noticed that the cross of pure-bred males on the mongrels results in progeny having one-half the blood of the pure-bred sires and one half the blood of the mongrel females. The females of this generation are mated back to the purebred sires and this results in progeny having three fourths the blood of the pure-bred sires. This progeny (female) is mated back again and the resulting progeny carries seven eighths pure blood. Mated back in this fashion for six generations the resulting progeny will carry 63-64 pure blood. At the end of the third and fourth matings the flock will assume, to all outward appearances, pure-blood characteristics in keeping with the breed of the original sires, except in isolated cases where the pure-bred sires come from a mongrel breed (in color) such as the Blue Andalusians.

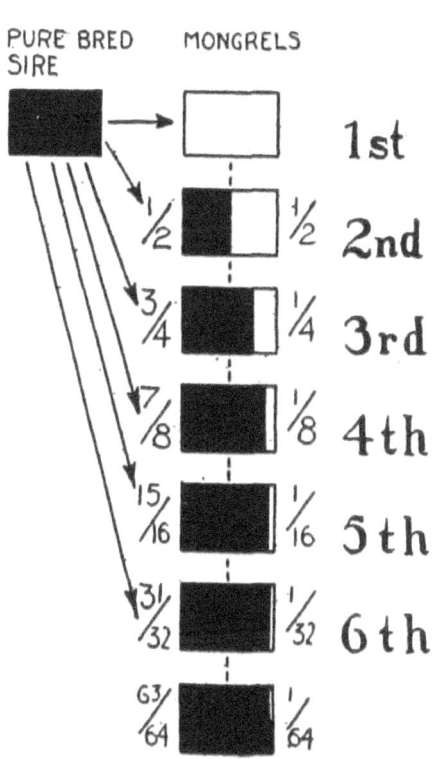

Fig. 42—Chart Showing Increase of Pure-blood Through Grading.

Grading has been generally neglected by the average farmer when it might have been of immense value to him in getting rid of a mongrel or indifferent flock without a violent interruption of the poultry work or a considerable outlay of cash. It can be used in crossing breeds, as well as in using standard-bred males of the same variety as the common flock of females. And it will demonstrate to anyone a most practical lesson of the power and weight of the laws of breeding, systematically and persistently carried out.

Selecting the Breeding Stock

The most important work by far confronting the farmer will be his selection of breeding stock. In our examination of the most fundamental of the laws of breeding we have already found that the individual characteristics of the breeding stock play a tremendous part in the practical work of breeding. One must first understand the fundamentals of breeding, then select the individuals best suited to achieve the purpose we have in mind, through the application of said principles.

Breeding is too often haphazardly gone about on the farm, and this accounts for the disappointment commonly met with. We cannot overemphasize the value and importance of careful selection. Upon it depends the success of any intelligent system of breeding. The farmer or breeder should know his stock; he should know it intimately and be fully acquainted with every detailed characteristic in order to properly judge the value of the individual for breeding purposes; then he must weigh the characteristics of the males against the females and determine in his mind, through his knowledge of the fundamentals of breeding, the probable effect of such-and-such a mating. This calls for painstaking work, as we have already indicated, but it is important work and the reward is worthy the effort. Mistakes of judgment will be made, in the nature of things, but the careful breeder will profit by his mistakes and capitalize them. He will, in the end, make progress.

The farmer is chiefly concerned in the selection of breeding stock for high fecundity, or egg production. He will need to become acquainted with the characteristics of the good layer, which are set out in detail in the chapter on Culling Farm Poultry for Any Purpose. But he should not go to extremes in this direction, as so many breeders are. One cannot long disregard standard qualities at

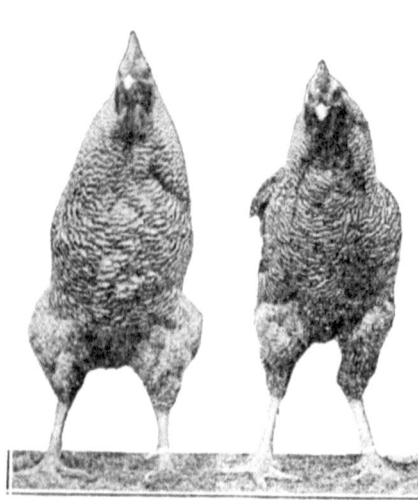

Fig. 43—Which would you select to head the breeding pen? Cock on left is the best bird, as he has better type to sire high-producing pullets.

CHAPTER V

the expense of high-laying ability, for there is slight justification in the idea that one must be sacrificed to gain the other. Recent breeding work at the Government Poultry Farm in Maryland has demonstrated that it is possible by proper selection and line breeding to produce a strain of high-record layers having also outstanding standard qualities.

The tide has started to run in that direction and it strongly indicates that the breeders who reap the large rewards in the future will be those who stick to the standard type as much as possible. This means that the farmer is going to have to study the standard qualifications of his breed as set out in the Standard of Perfection and to breed as closely to it as possible in his search for high fecundity. One can, of course, disregard it entirely, as the breeders of Tom Barron and English Leghorns have done and continue to secure high yields, but the trimmer and more efficient standard-bred fowl is bound to supplant them when it is more generally known that they can be bred to as high a state of fecundity. And the demand for stock, eggs and chicks, an important source of income even to market egg breeders, will be worth catering to.

There is an egg type in fowls and a beef type just as there is a dairy and beef type in cattle. The farmer must learn to distinguish these types. One of the outstanding characteristics of the heavy layer, not a sure index in every case but an important one nevertheless, is that they are usually under standard weight. Some of the best laying Leghorn pullets, for instance, weigh as low as three and one-half pounds. Careful weight records of high layers of all breeds and varieties at recent contests indicate that the tendency to be under weight is extremely pronounced in these birds, the average running from one and one-half to two pounds under standard weight. This does not mean that something is inherently wrong with the high-record layers; it may indicate, on the other hand, that the standard weight is too high for good layers.

The egg type is clearly set out in detail in the chapter on culling, but it is worth while to note herewith that the general characteristics of the egg type is as follows: Close feathering, thin pelvic bones, long backs, a tendency to high tails, great abdominal capacity, well spread legs, active, energetic, pale legs, bright and large combs and wattles.

For general stamina and vigor, select well-proportioned birds; the early hatched and matured generally being the most desirable for breeders; birds as close to standard type and conformity as possible. Vigor can generally be discovered by the simple expedient of watching the actions of the birds and in sticking to breed type. The first birds off the roost in the morning, the last to go to roost at night, the birds with large appetites, are the strongest in constitutional vigor, as a rule. Birds that are slow to mature, slow in the molting process, sluggish and of fair appetite may be discarded for breeding purposes.

Another indication, where the flock is bred up by selection by external characteristics, is in the matter of molting. Early molters are not, contrary to general opinion, the hens to keep for breeders. They are not the best layers. Select the late molters, for this carries the surest indication that they are the best layers in the flock.

CHAPTER VI

Care of the Farm Flock Breeding Pen

Isolate the Breeding Pen— Feeding for Fertile Eggs— Selection AND Care of Hatching Eggs— Fertility and Hatchability OF Eggs— Trap-Nesting and Pedigreeing

We have indicated in the preceding chapter that progress in breeding comes largely through the selection of individuals with reference to their characteristics which are desirable to attain the object the breeder has in mind. Flock breeding or mass breeding can never be a success, in the large sense, for the reason that the progress of the entire flock is limited by the quality of the worst specimens in it. In other words, the progeny can seldom do better than that of the average of the flock from which it springs.

The farmer has just two choices in his breeding work. He can use flock or mass breeding, as the majority of farmers have done for decades, or he can use breeding by selection, with an opportunity for advancement in the direction in which he goes.

If progress is desired, and it is unthinkable that it should not be desired, then the breeding flock which has been carefully and painstakingly selected, must be isolated from the rest of the flock and eggs set only from this carefully selected breeding pen or pens. Through this one avenue alone the farmer may vastly improve his flock, whether his object be egg production, market fowls or show stock.

The breeding pen should be composed of about 15 females and one male for the small egg breeds and about eight females and one male for the other breeds, for the very best results. Of course, one can vary this up or down as may be desired, but the chances for other factors to enter in, if the size of the breeding pen is increased, such as infertility or weak germs, do not make it advisable. Specialty breeders generally designate four females and one male "a, breeding pen," when selling stock to beginners.

The pen should be housed in a compact, dry, well-ventilated, damp and draft proof coop, such as was recommended in the chapter on buildings for this purpose. The coop need not be large in size, it need not be expensive or ornamental in construction. A fenced yard or run may or may not be provided, just as conditions seem to warrant. The breeders cannot be allowed to run in this yard in weather if the best egg yield is to be expected from them, or if clean eggs for incubation purposes are to be secured from them. Where the house is ample, well-ventilated, and the hens are properly fed and cared for, no outside yard or run will be necessary for the production of strong, fertile eggs.

Fig. 44—A Farm Flock Breeding Pen Where Mass Breeding Is Followed.

Only fully matured stock should be used in the breeding pen. Too many people in their anxiety to rush matters and "cash in" on the profits they have in mind, resort to the use of pullets in the breeding pen at a time when they are not fully matured. We have not satisfied ourselves that there is any valid objection to the use of good, strong, well-matured pullets in the breeding pen when yearlings are not available, but the pullets should not be used until rather late in their pullet year as breeders because before that time they are not sufficiently matured to lay a good egg, for incubating purposes.

The best results come from the yearling hens which lay a larger egg than pullets, a more uniform egg in size and weight and an egg that will hatch a larger chick than those from pullet eggs. The yearlings selected from the pullet flock of the previous year for breeding purposes, should be selected early in the winter and isolated from the main laying flock in order that they may be free from any forcing rations, artificial lighting or other methods immediately preceding the time when their eggs are desired for hatching purposes. Hens that have not been forced to exert themselves unduly for high records during the present season will give the best results in the breeding pen.

CHAPTER VI

Feeding for Fertile Eggs

The breeding pen must have different rations and care from that given the laying flock. The care differs only in respect to the tendency to force the laying hens. This should not be done in the case of the breeders, everything on the contrary, being done to make conditions as natural, comfortable and attractive as possible.

Forcing ingredients in the ration must be omitted. This includes green cut bone, tankage, beef scraps, bacon cracklings, raw meat or any other form of meat scraps ordinarily fed for forcing heavy egg production. We do not mean to imply that the breeder will not produce fertile eggs if fed meat or beef scraps of certain kinds in judicious quantities in the ration. "We are speaking in general terms because experience has shown that most of these elements may be at the bottom of infertile eggs or eggs showing poor hatchability. Fresh, raw lean meat is excellent for breeding hens, but it is so seldom that it can or will be fed in this condition that it should be ruled out, in a general statement. Green cut bone should be barred absolutely from the rations of breeders because it results in poor fertility and hatchability of the eggs. The same objection applies to tankage and meat scraps, but in less degree. If they are fed in limited quantities, they will do no harm.

The best ration for breeding fowls is one made up entirely of clean, wholesome grains and ingredients, supplemented by green food. The latter is almost an absolute necessity, as in the case of laying hens. It does much to promote the good health of the fowls and is eagerly devoured by them. As a general rule, do not feed heavily of it, as one would to layers on a full forcing ration. Excessive quantities also acts on the bowels.

Grit, charcoal, shell and water should be before the hens at all times. The importance of these cannot be over-emphasized. Shell, especially, and water play an important part in egg production and unless the hens have sufficient shell they are not likely to lay perfectly formed eggs, so desirable for incubating purposes.

A simple and very satisfactory ration for the breeding pens, which we have used several seasons is as follows: Mash (for winter feeding), wheat bran, two parts; corn meal, two parts; ground oats, one part, and alfalfa meal, as much as the hens can be induced to eat. If the mash is moistened with milk and water and fed fresh each time, the hens will eat as much as four parts of the alfalfa meal in the mash. In addition, use one part wheat middlings in the mash mixture.

This is supplemented with whole oats, cracked corn and buckwheat or wheat, sprouted oats or other green food, lean fresh meat if possible, otherwise sweet milk. Feed the oats, buckwheat and wheat lightly in the litter in the morning and the cracked corn at night with wheat, two parts of the corn to one of wheat. The proper amount of sprouted oats per hen, after they have become accustomed to them is two ounces per hen once a day. It is not necessary to weigh them each feeding, but it is a good plan to weigh them up for the pen at the start so that you get an accurate idea of the amount in bulk. In starting to feed sprouted oats commence with one ounce per hen and gradually increase the amount until you have them on full feed.

Whole oats and dry wheat bran in hoppers before the hens all the time is an excellent plan where the fertile egg mash is fed moistened. This will be a valuable supplement. If plenty of bran and sprouted oats or other green food is furnished, one can dispense with the fresh lean beef or meat scraps entirely. Commercial beef scraps composed entirely of lean meat will not injure the hatching quality of the eggs, but where it is not composed of lean scraps it will have some effect upon the quality for hatching purposes.

Selection and Care of Hatching Eggs

Good, common sense should indicate to anyone at all acquainted with eggs the kind and type to select for incubation. If no other rule than that of selecting the largest and most perfect eggs were followed, there would be slight criticism to be made. For such a plan would be a good one and secure the results desired in the majority of cases.

Irregular, imperfect, misshapen eggs should not be selected for hatching purposes. Eggs with "rings around them" or ridges in the shells seldom, if ever, hatch good chicks. There are variations in the size and perfection of eggs as well as in breed type or color markings and the careful breeder will not breed from hens showing these characteristics. Small eggs, it should be kept in mind, will produce small chicks that are very likely to be handicapped from the very start, although this is not always the case. On the other hand, excessively large eggs are no more desirable for hatching purposes.

CHAPTER VI

Fig. 45—Ideal Quarters for Breeding Pen.

The nice, smooth, perfectly formed eggs of uniform size and weight, striking a golden mean between the two extremes, are the desirable eggs for incubation. Sometimes they will weigh 26 to 28 ounces to the dozen and, again, they will average 30 ounces. It is safe to say that the majority of eggs best suited for incubation purposes will weigh between 26 and 30 ounces per dozen. Small pullet eggs are not ordinarily desirable. We have purchased eggs from specialty breeders at a long price and been disappointed when they arrived and were found to be small pullet eggs, but the results, in one case at least, turned out to be exceptionally fine. This is stated merely to show that there are exceptions to all rules, but these exceptions only serve to prove the rule. The fact remains that small eggs or pullet eggs of small size should not be set as a general proposition.

It would seem that anyone, on taking thought, should know that certain practices which are indulged in saving eggs for hatching are likely to interfere with the best results from the eggs. People, however, are subject to carelessnesses which penalize them and seldom take thought until trouble arises. Hatching eggs that are carefully selected from stock in turn carefully selected represent the fruit of painstaking effort. They are too valuable to be needlessly impaired in their value.

The very best way to handle hatching eggs is to set them the same day they are laid. The longer the eggs are held, the less valuable they will be and the smaller the size of the chick hatched, due to the evaporation of the moisture in the egg. "Where the breeding pens are of sufficient size to furnish enough eggs to incubate every day or two, the quality of the chicks will be found to be a great deal better than where the eggs are kept even a week after being laid.

It is possible to hatch chicks from eggs several weeks old, but it is not advisable to attempt it. There is slight reason why the farmer should hold his eggs more than one week for hatching purposes. If his incubator is too large, it will pay him to buy two or three small machines for the special purpose of hatching his eggs. If he has a number of small machines, say of 50-egg capacity, he can resort to pedigree breeding by the simple expedient of setting the eggs from one pen in one of the machines and those from another pen in another machine. If he has a mammoth machine, he can follow the same plan by starting a tray at a time.

Eggs kept for hatching purposes that are not set immediately should be turned every day, but once each day is sufficient and they should be handled gently. Rough turning is not necessary and it is claimed by some experts that frequent turning injures the albumen. The eggs should be kept in a temperature of less than 50 degrees in order to prevent the rapid evaporation of moisture that takes place in cases where the temperature is over that figure.

They should be kept in flat trays and not in the "patent" egg cabinets one so often sees where the eggs are placed upright on the small end. Eggs should lie in their natural position, which is flat, just as they do in the nest or in the incubator trays. To stand them on the small end places the germ in an improper position and interferes with normal development.

Fertility and Hatchability op Eggs

Not all fertile eggs will hatch chicks and riot all chicks that hatch will be strong and vigorous enough to develop into the kind of fowls desired. The question of fertility and hatchability of eggs is one which has challenged the best thought of breeders and experimental scientists for many years. It is not yet certain that we know all the factors influencing this question, but we do know a great many things which have a bearing upon the subject.

Fertility is almost entirely a question resting with the male bird. It is seldom, indeed, that a male heading a breeding pen, that has gone through the several processes necessary in careful selection before he attains that position, will be constitutionally incapable of properly fertilizing the eggs, although it does occur now and then. It seems that the feeding of breeders has a tremendous influence upon the hatchability of the eggs, and improper care and housing conditions may also play their part in weakening the germs, but a sterile male is a very rare occurrence.

A number of breeders have reported that eggs from a breeding flock which did not hatch, but that contained chicks at the start of the test, can soon be changed in inherent character by the simple expedient of changing the feeding ration along the lines suggested in a preceding paragraph. One breeder states that within three weeks after changing the ration he was able to secure hatching eggs from a breeding pen that produced good, strong chicks, while the eggs before the ration was changed would not hatch. This indicates that the feeding and care was at fault.

Just what influence the weather has upon the hatchability and fertility of hatching eggs has not been accurately determined, so far as we know, but it does seem to have an effect. In cold, raw spring weather we have noticed a general complaint about the fertility of eggs, not only in general farm flocks, but among the flocks of commercial poultrymen. In one season recently, the best hatches we had records of were around 50 per cent. Anyone will recognize that this is ordinarily a very low percentage. Proper rations, housing and care did not seem to correct entirely the adverse effect of the weather. Just what this effect is, or what the cause of it is, we are unable to state.

Strong, vigorous male birds must be selected for the breeding pens and due reference given to their age and probable breeding value. If a male bird is old and apparently has his best service behind him, he should be mated to a very few females, less than the ordinary number, for the best results. Sometimes poor fertility or hatchability is due to the attempt to make the male bird serve too many females. One farmer has written us within the past few days in which he stated that he has used only four males to 200 hens the past few seasons and that his fertility has averaged over 95 per cent for each year. All the comment we can make upon this is that he has been extremely fortunate. It is seldom, if indeed ever, that any such results can be expected from male birds.

The proportion of males to females to use for the best results is one male to 10 or 15 females in the egg breeds such as Leghorns, Campines and Minorcas, and one male to seven or eight females in the heavier breeds such as Plymouth Rocks, Wyandottes and Reds is as high a proportion as can be counted upon to give the best results. The size of the breeding flock also has an important effect upon the fertility to be obtained from a given number of males. It may seem to be contradictory to say that the larger the flock the less the number of males required, and the smaller the flock the larger the number of males required, but it is true, nevertheless.

Every breeder can determine the question to his own satisfaction by testing the fertility of eggs from breeding pens by checking the results obtained from different pens against each other. If he is using trap-nests and is pedigreeing, he will soon learn a great deal about the individual characteristics of different hens in the breeding pens. He will find that some hens throw an unusually large proportion of clear or infertile eggs; that other hens, while exceptionally high layers, are poor breeders, and that hens having the highest percentage of fertile eggs often have a low percentage of hatchability. As soon as characteristics of this nature are discovered, and they seem to be due to the hen rather than to other considerations, it is wise to eliminate these individuals from the breeding pens, because the chances are that the characteristics are hereditary and are likely to be transmitted. This is especially true in the case of hens showing poor fertility of eggs laid.

The handling of the hatching eggs has an effect upon the hatchability which should be reasonably apparent to all. No matter how strong the germ in the egg, it can be materially weakened by improper handling not only prior to incubation, but during the process.

Improper turning of the eggs during incubation, imperfect moisture control, and lack of adequate cooling of the eggs all seriously affect the hatchability of eggs. Eggs that are not cooled or turned at all during the process of incubation will develop very poor hatches, as compared with eggs that have been properly handled, every other consideration being absolutely equal. The temperature in which the eggs are cooled has an effect upon the value of the cooling and must be regulated in time accordingly. Recommendations along this line will be found in the Chapter on Incubation and should be carefully followed for the best results.

Plenty of green food in the ration improves the fertility and hatchability of eggs and should not be denied the breeders. Moisture control and cooling tend to weaken the shell fiber so that the chicks can escape at the proper time, and must be taken care of, if results are to be obtained.

CHAPTER VI

Bulky elements in the mash ration are especially valuable in promoting fertility and hatchability, as recommended elsewhere in this chapter.

Trap-Nesting and Pedigreeing

The greatest value of the trap-nest comes in its use in the breeding pen, where it makes pedigreeing possible. There are objections, serious objections, to the general us of the trap-nest by farmers in large flocks because of the close and confining attention they demand. Commercial breeders who are spending their entire time in the business cannot well afford to do without the trap-nest from the day the pullets go into the laying houses until they are disposed of, because it is the one sure road to progress and profit.

Fig. 46—An Excellent Breeding Pen of White Wyandottes. Pedigree Breeding Is Easily Practiced with Small Fens.

The farmer, however, can spot the desirable laying type hens and pullets by the external methods of culling, some of which are exceedingly efficient and accurate. He can select the pullets to go into the laying houses by this method and then can select the breeders for the next season, at the end of the first laying year, by the simple process of picking the most desirable individuals in type and station, giving due reference to the culling points found valuable in choosing the good layers. These methods will not be as certain of finding the exceptional hens in each flock, but they will insure some progress and get away from the heavy liability imposed by general trapnesting.

But the small, carefully selected breeding pen, which is isolated from the rest of the laying flock, which is small in numbers should, by all means, be trap-nested during the breeding season in order that pedigree breeding may be used.

Pedigree breeding is nothing mysterious and not laborious with a small breeding pen. It is simply the keeping of an accurate record of the parentage of each chick so that the records of performance may be checked up, in an effort to locate the prepotent individuals in the flock from which to base future matings. The actual mechanics of pedigree breeding are based upon the trapnest and no one has a right to claim that he is pedigree breeding who is not using the trap-nest.

The process may be described as follows: As soon as a hen is taken from the trap-nest, her leg band number is written on the egg she has laid so as to identify it. A record is kept of the laying performance of each hen in the pen in order to furnish an index of her probable yearly record. The eggs from the different hens in the breeding pen are either incubated under different hens, in different compartments of the incubator or in different machines. Where they are all incubated together, the eggs from the same hens should be placed in coarse cheese-cloth sacks just before they are ready to pip so that the chicks after they escape from the shells do not become mixed. As soon as they are dry and are taken from the machine or from under the different hens, they are given a distinctive toe punch and that toe punch is entered on the record of their dams. The sire is the male heading the whole pen, or it may be an individual sire, as where individual matings are made.

In this way the percentage of the various chicks produced from the breeding pen is preserved and can be used for future reference in mating up future breeding pens. The performance of different progeny will be found to excel that of other progeny; it will be found that the male mated to a certain hen will produce exceptional pullets, while mated to another hen, he may produce exceptional cockerels, and some matings will produce nothing of value at all. The whole value of pedigreeing is that it serves to clear up the work and to remove the necessity of the breeder working entirely in the dark as to his breeding operations.

CHAPTER VII

Natural and Artificial Incubation

Hatching With Hens— The Modern Incubator for Hatching — How to Handle the Incubator— Mammoth. Incubators AND Their Management— Running a Hatchery

Hatching with hens on the farm has been a comparatively common practice until within the last few years. It is still in common practice on many farms where small flocks are produced each year for home consumption. But hatching with hens is of slight economic importance on those farms where any serious attention is given to the farm flock. The labor element involved, the large loss in chicks bound to occur through accident or otherwise under this system, the constant necessity of fighting lice and mites attacking the chicks through the hens, are the chief reasons. Another reason, one that is often the controlling reason, is the fact that it is impossible to produce a large and uniform flock of youngsters, such as is necessary where a large number of layers is desired each year, by this method.

There is no weight to be given to the old and widespread idea that hens only can hatch good, strong chicks. As a matter of fact, the hen today is not as efficient an incubating agency as the modern incubator. This may agitate some people, but it is nevertheless a fact. The hen can never be absolutely depended upon by the attendant; she may escape from the nest and remain away for hours at the critical period; she may become unruly and tramp the whole setting into a mass of broken and blasted hopes, and she has an unhappy faculty of stepping on the largest and best chicks and killing them through her clumsiness. The management of an incubator may scare some people, but no incubator in the world ever offered as much potential trouble as an ordinary setting hen.

No doubt there are good and efficient setting hens which make excellent mothers. If they can be economically used to incubate hatching eggs, there is no reason why they should be discarded, but we feel that the surest chance of the greatest profit and the least cost in incubation lies in the direction of the incubator and the brooder.

Where hens are to be used for hatching, some general observations will be in order. In the first place, do not make the mistake of setting the first hens to become broody in the spring. These hens are the best and most efficient layers in the whole flock because they are the ones that have been laying all winter. If the farmer dispenses with their services in the laying flock and permits them to incubate his hatching eggs, he will, in fact, be setting eggs from the poorest layers in the flock and hatching them with the best layers. The poorest layers, the ones that have loafed all winter and started to lay only when spring weather comes on are the drones of the flock and the farmer is unwittingly a party to propagating his flock from the least valuable individuals in it.

Provide the hens that are set with a nice, roomy nest in a quiet, secluded spot where they will not be molested by the other hens. It is a mistake to set them in the hen house where every other cranky hen can have a chance to bother them.

An empty orange crate, which can be secured at any grocery store, makes an ideal nest for setting hens. Each crate will accommodate two hens. Take one of the slats off the side (the top one) and place a layer of paper on the bottom and a nice nest of excelsior or clean straw on top. Some people take a strip of grass sod and turn it upside down and place it in the nest, but we can see no particular advantage in the practice. Ordinary straw or clean excelsior will make a fine nest.

It is true that one does not have to fill lamps, adjust regulators or shovel coal when hatching with hens, but it is likewise true that one has to feed the hen, see that she gets some exercise, that lice are kept down, and that she doesn't stay off the nest too long. This, in turn, requires time and attention amounting to as much or more than incubators require.

The Modern Incubator fob Hatching

It is not necessary for us to advance any reasons in favor of the modern incubator. It has proved its own case so conclusively to the thousands of commercial poultrymen and to hundreds of thousands of farmers and small flock raisers all over the country. The overwhelming majority of all commercial flocks are replenished every year from incubator chicks hatched from eggs laid by hens in turn hatched in incubators.

CHAPTER VII

The incubator has been perfected to such a high state as an efficient hatching machine that it is now possible to produce greater uniformity in chicks, and to hatch better chicks, than can be hatched by hens. This is what might be called a bald statement, but it is unquestionably true. Better chicks are hatched today in the average mammoth incubator, properly handled, than can be hatched by hens. This is due to the fact that the moisture problem is scientifically regulated and by application of every automatic and scientific principle necessary the maximum results are obtained from the egg.

We are perfectly aware of the fact that many people secure poor results from their attempts to hatch chicks from incubators. The first two or three hatches are very apt to be disappointing in results, simply because the operator is unfamiliar with all the details necessary for success, and forgets or leaves out something. Conditions that may influence hatches where small machines are used do not occur as frequently in the large mammoth machines because everything possible is automatically controlled. Even alarm systems are installed on these machines to warn the operator when the temperature goes down too low or up too high. This would be, of course, impracticable in the small machine. The regulation of the moisture supply, and the temperature, rests almost entirely upon individual judgment, allowing an opportunity for the novice to make mistakes.

But these are speedily overcome by those who use common sense and make an effort to understand what they are about and how to obtain the best results. The incubator is not a producer of weak, puny chicks of limited constitutional vigor. If it does produce such chicks, one of two things have occurred: Either the machine has not been operated absolutely according to directions or else the breeding stock or the way in which the breeding stock has been handled is at fault.

Some judgment should be exercised in buying the incubator. There is a wide choice offered the farmer, and machines can be secured at almost any price to fit the purse. Cheap machines are almost invariably selected by beginners and it requires, as a rule, more skill to secure good hatches from such machines than from machines more carefully and painstakingly manufactured.

One need not necessarily select the highest-priced machine on the market, but there is generally a reason why some machines cost more than others. One may be certain that that reason is not the increased profits of the manufacturer, for stiff competition tends to prevent an unreasonable profit. The difference in price is largely due to the difference in the cost of materials going into the machine and the care with which it is put together.

The first cost is not the sole criterion of value in any appliance and this is just as true of incubators as of anything else. A machine cheap in first cost, if it will not give the best of results for its purpose, is the most expensive machine that can be bought. Machines that admit of imperfect and haphazard regulation, that are made of improperly seasoned material and have a tendency of sucking moisture out of eggs as a sponge takes up water, are not to be recommended. Use care in selecting your incubator, giving due reference to your needs and to the future.

Most people buy machines too small in size. They do not plan for the future. If there is any thought at all of expanding in the immediate future, it will pay to buy as large a machine as possible to take care of the needs you have in mind. This will eliminate the accumulation of a number of smaller machines, which increase the labor of management as many times as there are machines. Then, again, incubators will seldom accommodate as many eggs as they are rated. A machine rated to accommodate 120 eggs will seldom handle more than 100 eggs and due allowance should be made in this direction.

How TO Handle the Incubator

The best place to operate the incubator is unquestionably in a cellar. A place must be selected where the average temperature does not greatly fluctuate, because this makes it difficult to maintain an even temperature in the machine. Where a room in the residence is selected the tendency is to heat up during the day and to cool down the temperature during the night. This outside temperature has an effect upon the temperature in the machine and makes it extremely difficult, especially in days of changeable weather outside, to keep the temperature where it belongs in the machine. If no cellar is available, select a room where there is the least fluctuation of temperature at all times as the most satisfactory in which to secure the best results. This is especially important because it will be found extremely difficult in the fluctuating warm and cold weather in spring, when cold snaps are likely to come, to maintain the temperature.

CHAPTER VII

The machine should be leveled up so that the egg chamber is perfectly level. This is necessary in order that there may be a uniform distribution of heat in all parts of the chamber. If the machine is not level, it will be found that different parts of the egg chamber will be maintaining different temperatures. One can demonstrate the truth of this statement by placing a number of thermometers in different parts of the chamber. The best way to level the machine will be to use an ordinary carpenter's level.

The next point is to fill the lamp and start the machine. Run it for several days, in the meantime carefully adjusting the regulator screw until it is maintaining an even temperature. It is best not to attempt the regulation of the machine until the egg chamber is thoroughly heated. This will require several hours. Adjust the machine to an average, full, well-rounded flame and after the machine is regulated do not change the regulator screw, but increase or diminish the temperature in the egg chamber by increasing or diminishing the size of the flame. The fact that the regulator arm rises rapidly after the eggs are put in the machine or after cooling the eggs should not be a cause for alarm or an immediate changing of the regulation, because this is a tendency that is bound to occur. Soon it will settle down and the egg chamber temperature will then come up to the proper point before the regulator permanently rises.

The most persistent tendency on the part of people running incubators for the first time, which seriously interferes with the chances of a successful hatch, is the tendency to "tinker" with the regulator during the hatch. It is this one temptation which ruins more hatches and causes more of the so-called "incubator" chicks to be brought into the world than anything else. The operator should have the courage of his convictions and be willing to give the machine a fair chance to produce. If he is worried and convinced that the regulation needs to be adjusted, it will pay him to keep a close watch on the machine for several hours and if no change in temperature has been made, then he may properly change it to the desired point, but this will seldom, if ever, occur when the machine has been properly regulated in the first instance.

Where the temperature has, for some unaccountable reason, gotten up several degrees too high, it can be quickly lowered by sprinkling lukewarm water lightly over the eggs, but this should not be done persistently or it will decrease the size of the chicks hatched. The greatest danger is from overheated eggs, while where the temperature has been under the proper point for a few hours there is little to be worried about after the first week, but it should be brought up as quickly as possible.

The lamps should be trimmed and filled every morning rather than at night, because there is a tendency, as everyone knows who has used kerosene lamps or lanterns, for the flame to "creep up" half an hour or so after it has been adjusted, and this will necessitate lowering the flame a good many times during the hatch. If the lamps were not taken care of until night there would be more of a chance of the flame running up too high a temperature in the machine and causing damage during the night. Use a high grade of kerosene because it contains less carbon and is less likely to smoke and catch fire. It is also more economical because it will deliver more heat and will not require as much to carry through a hatch as the cheaper grades. Sometimes it is almost impossible to maintain an even temperature with cheap grades of kerosene. The lamps should always be trimmed and filled after the eggs have been turned and cooled, because the presence of kerosene on the hands is very apt to cause trouble. It has been said on good authority that the presence of kerosene on the shell will kill the chick within.

One should commence to turn the eggs after the third day and they should then be turned twice a day until the first egg is pipped. Frequent turning of the eggs during the process of incubation will have a beneficial rather than a detrimental effect. If one watches a hen on the nest it will be noticed that she not only turns the eggs twice a day, but several times. It has been demonstrated in the author's own experience that eggs turned frequently, at least three times a day, will hatch much better than eggs turned only once or twice a day. It is not the mere turning that produces the beneficial results, although that is important, but it is the contraction caused by the change of atmosphere, which plays an important part in breaking down the fiber of the shell and rendering it easier for the chick to escape at the proper time.

The eggs should also be cooled once each day in addition to the cooling they receive when being turned. The great purpose of cooling is to strengthen the chick and to produce the beneficial result on the shell that we have already mentioned. There are some authorities who are beginning to question whether or not it is necessary to cool the eggs, but for our own part we are not willing to give up or advise the giving up of the

CHAPTER VII

practice. Anyone who cares to experiment can demonstrate to himself the value of cooling by refraining from cooling one hatching of eggs. He will be surprised at the difference in results due to the cooling process. Various rules are given for the length of time in which to cool the eggs. We have found that since the temperature of the room always varies somewhat that it is a better plan to follow the simple index of placing the hands on the eggs and as soon as they appear cool, they should be returned to the machine. Note we say cool, not cold. As the hatch progresses, this will require more time, which is desirable.

The eggs should be tested as soon as possible and all infertiles and dead germs removed in order to give the room to the others. While-shelled eggs can be tested in four or five days after being placed in the machine for infertiles, while brown-shelled eggs can seldom be tested before the seventh day and oftentimes not until later, due to the inability to see through the shell. There are many methods of testing eggs, but we have found a simple way which is a time-saver and should commend itself to every poultryman. Simply pull out the egg tray and run an electric flash-light around under the tray close to the under side of the eggs. The infertiles and dead germs can then be lifted out with the other hand. It is not necessary to handle all the eggs in order to find the undesirables.

Another method is to set the tray on the edges of two chairs and run the flash-light around under the tray. Any number of methods will suggest themselves to the operator. One good plan is to simply place the egg between the two hands and hold it up to a strong light, turning slowly.

All eggs that are perfectly clear are discarded as being infertile and eggs having decidedly dark rings around the embryo are also thrown away because they are imperfectly fertilized and will not hatch chicks. Eggs which seem to be imperfectly developed or considerably behind the average in their development may also be taken out so that the others may have the room.

It is a good plan to crack open the eggs that are discarded, place them in separate saucers and examine them. One can get a better grasp of the development of the embryo through this method than any other that we might suggest. Experience of this sort will reveal many things to the incubator operator. For instance, if one cares to make the experiment, it will be found that eggs carried at a low temperature develop chicks that have a hard time getting out of the shell, especially where the temperature is carried too low the first week. Too much cooling the first week will cause the same condition. The chicks produced will be "sticky" and stick to the shell and anything else they come in contact with, and they generally hatch a day or two late. If any irregularity in the temperature is to be had it is better to run it too high than too low. If run two degrees too high the chicks will hatch early, but they will have a better chance than those retarded by low temperatures or too frequent cooling the first week. Where the temperature is run too high it will tend to cause the yolk to harden and the chick after taking it into its system will be unable to digest it. These chicks seldom live more than a week after being hatched.

The correct temperature to maintain is largely a matter for the manufacturer of your machine to dictate. He understands his machine and knows from his experience just what it should be. Various manufacturers differ in their recommendations in this respect. Some suggest that the temperature be carried at 102 degrees the first week, 103 degrees the second week and 103 1/2 degrees the third week, while others suggest 102, 103 and 104, respectively. No set rule can be announced. That is for the manufacturer of your machine to indicate.

Mammoth Incubators and Their Management

The actual process of incubation of eggs in mammoth machines is not materially different than in the ordinary machines. The chief point of difference is that the mammoth machines handle considerably more eggs at but slightly increased cost of hatching than the smaller, lamp-heated machines. Ten thousand eggs at one hatching from a single machine is not an uncommon occurrence with mammoth machines.

The mammoth machine has rendered possible to the poultry world the same advantages automatic machinery brought to the farmer in other lines. The ordinary incubator made it possible for the farmer and the poultryman to increase his output at slight additional cost over the handling of the setting hen; the mammoth machine has, in turn, done the same thing for the man who found it hard to carry on his business with a large number of smaller machines.

The mammoth incubators are unusually efficient hatching machines. It is a singular fact that in visiting with farmers and poultrymen all over the Middle West the past 10 years that we have never encountered a single one owning a mammoth machine, regardless of make, that was dissat-

CHAPTER VII

isfied or who felt that better results could be obtained with smaller machines or setting hens. The exact reverse is, on the other hand, true. Practically every one stated that the mammoth machine gave better results than they had ever experienced before.

There is one outstanding desirable feature of the mammoth machines which should appeal to all. They can be purchased in small units or sections and expand as the business grows, new sections being added to the same circuit and receiving its heat from the same heater. The mammoth machines generally require the construction of special incubator cellars, if the cellar to the residence is not available or large enough. This can be done economically, however, by building the brooder house above and the same heating plants can be made to do double service.

As to the actual mechanics of running the mammoth incubator, there is little detailed advice that we can give. Practically every machine operates on a principle slightly different from its nearest competitor and each machine must be handled in a manner peculiar only to it. This is especially true in the case of the heating apparatus.

The best advice that can be offered is to give full faith and credit to the manufacturer's instructions. He knows more about the manner in which the machine should be operated for the best results than Dick Jones, or Tom Brown, the interested neighbors.

Be particularly careful to maintain the manufacturer's directions in regard to the temperature that is to be maintained in the egg chambers. Very often they recommend that the temperature be brought to 103 degrees as soon as possible after the eggs have been placed in the machine and that temperature maintained as evenly as possible throughout the hatch. While this is contrary to the general advice given in the management of incubators, it is best to do as the manufacturer recommends. We have personally, in experiments, maintained an even temperature of 103 degrees throughout the entire hatch in small machines and have had satisfactory results. The reason we happened to do this was because we were pedigree hatching by placing different eggs in the machines two or three days apart and we felt that it would be better for all the eggs to maintain an even temperature throughout than to try to fluctuate it. One can resort to this plan, but it will be found that 103 degrees is a little too hot the first few days and to maintain that temperature is to lose a few more chicks that otherwise would be the case due to too rapid development of the embryo at first.

Running a Hatchery

There is a very good profit to be made at the present time in the baby chick business, especially where the hatchery is supplied with eggs from a flock maintained right on the place. The time is coming when the commercial hatcheries are going to find it increasingly hard to secure business because they have lost the confidence of the poultry buying public.

In the days when they had the field to themselves they did not hesitate, in order to supply the great demand for baby chicks, to hatch eggs from flocks of indifferent bred fowls and sell them as pure-bred— to buy up eggs here, there and everywhere and advertise them as coming from certain strains popular in the public mind; other unscrupulous individuals organized fake hatcheries, took orders for baby chicks and then politely pocketed the money. We do not mean to say that all the commercial hatcheries were guilty of dishonest practices, for this is not true, but there were a sufficient number of dishonest people masquerading under the title "hatchery" to make the public at large unwary of the whole outfit.

The real sincere hatchery operators are operating and always have operated their own breeding flocks, many of them maintaining a number of separate farms on which to carry on their breeding work. But the temper of the times is commencing to be and will be more so in the future, to buy as much from actual poultry breeders as possible.

This means that the farmer who is building up a good flock of laying hens for commercial egg purposes will be in a position to capitalize the demand and make an additional profit from his eggs in the spring months when market prices slump by marketing them in the form of baby chicks.

All that the farmer or small poultryman needs to realize on this demand is sufficient hatching capacity to take care of the eggs produced for him by his flock of breeders. If he wishes to sell general utility stock, he can secure sufficient male birds to mate to his general laying flock and sell the entire yield during the spring months in the form of hatching eggs and baby chicks.

CHAPTER VII

This will call for a mammoth incubator, a good, well-bred flock of layers and breeders, and sufficient advertising to market the product. As a rule an advertisement run in state farm papers, local papers or a few poultry journals will furnish all the demand that can be supplied, if the price is right.

CHAPTER VIII

Successful Brooding of Chicks

Objects And Methods of Brooding— Fireless Brooders— Oil Lamp Brooders— Crude Oil Brooders— Portable Coal Hover Brooders— Brooder House Methods— Care of Chicks On Large Scale

There is no system of brooding that can be expected to exceed the hen in giving the chicks the proper brooding. If we can approximate the hen in the results obtained, then our method of brooding is a success whether it be an old box covered with blankets or the most expensive brooding equipment ever manufactured.

The constant effort is to give the chicks the care they would receive from the hen and to maintain these results in the face of large flocks of chicks often running to several thousand from a single hatch. The. first and primary object is to protect the chicks from chilling on the one hand and over-heating on the other. In other words, we must strive to keep the chicks comfortable regardless of the condition of the weather. Unless we do this, our losses are bound to be enormous.

The development of brooder equipment has kept pace with the progress made by the entire poultry industry in the past 15 years. A few years ago we used the old box brooders fed by a kerosene lamp, which were death traps to say the least. Most of them were square or oblong in shape with square corners, in which the chicks had an unreasonable habit of piling up at just the wrong time, tramping each other to death and "sweating" until those that did survive lost their feathers and were seriously stunted.

Then we rushed to the other extreme and resorted to the injurious use of tireless brooders and suffered more losses through piling up and crowding when a sudden cold snap came along. But out of the chaos that

Fig. 47—Outside Runs for Chicks in the Brooder House Strengthen Their Legs and Insure Better Development.

existed then there finally came the development of brooding systems which have afforded the poultryman depending upon artificial brooding methods a breathing spell. Appliances were developed which corrected the earlier evils of the lamp and box brooder and the attempt was made to forestall the tendencies of the chicks and correct the evils which had been responsible for these tendencies, thereby insuring better results with less attention and worry on the part of the attendant. We then had round brooders of the portable type, made of galvanized iron or other fireproof material, where the chicks could not pile up in the corners, and where the ventilation was given consideration so that the chicks would not smother to death so easily.

Later came the large canopy hovers, using both coal and crude oil which tended to make the brooding of large flocks of chicks possible at a single operation; then we had the hot water systems used in connection with the brooder houses, the portable coal hover brooder using a stove which furnished a more uniform and dependable heat than the small lamp flame brooders.

These large and portable brooders have revolutionized the handling of baby chicks just as the mammoth incubator revolutionized the hatching of eggs, They have made it possible for the commercial poultryman and the farmer to hatch their flocks of layers, whether 1,000 or 10,000 in one or two hatches, brood them at the same time and bring the whole flock to maturity at the very same time. The tremendous advantage of a flock of young pullets uniform in size and in development cannot well be over-estimated.

Dependable brooding equipment has also made possible early hatches at a season when natural brooding would be out of the question. This permits the commercial poultryman and the farmer to mature his pullets in time for the fall egg trade when prices commence to mount, and to market the surplus cockerels as broilers at the season of the year when prices are the highest.

Brooding equipment is dependable today, provided a reasonable amount of common sense is used in handling such appliances. The man who uses his head and who is on the job every day and often in the night need have no fear of the brooding equipment offered him today. "Eternal vigilance is the price of success" was never truer than in the case of brooding young chicks properly.

FIRELESS Brooders

Every now and then questions come to us from farmers asking for plans for building fireless brooders and whether or not they are a success. So far as we know, the fireless brooder gained its popularity largely through the widespread advocacy of the "Philo system" of raising poultry. Many people, especially people who are trying to raise large flocks of chicks, have been misled into thinking that it would be entirely practicable for their own needs and would be more economical than brooders requiring artificial heat.

The author has personally used fireless brooders for many years, and while he realizes their great worth and has proved to his own satisfaction that they are a distinct success under proper conditions, he does not recommend them for people who are brooding large flocks of chicks. The labor element involved is practically as great, in the case of large flocks, as the use of hens would be for a moderately-sized flock. The man with several thousand chicks, or several hundred for that matter, would be seriously handicapped by their use.

The fireless brooder is particularly valuable and does its best work when used on comparatively small flocks of chicks. While it is possible to brood 50 to 100 chicks in these brooders, depending upon their size, the first week, it is necessary to divide the chicks each week as they grow, in order to prevent over-heating and losses, and this means increasing the equipment and the labor necessary. For a flock of 50 to 100 chicks, however, they can be used to excellent advantage and will give wonderful results.

The fireless brooder cannot be used outside in cold weather. They must be used inside a brooder house, barn or shed where the temperature does not go down low enough during the day to chill the chicks. Used in connection with the "Philo system" brooder coops they are a distinct success even in chilly weather, but no commercial poultryman or farmer can afford to utilize that system. It is primarily a system of intensive poultry for back-lotters and town people.

A fireless brooder can be constructed in a few minutes by anyone handy with a saw and hammer. Make the box 18 inches square and 10 inches high. Cut a door in one side and place it on hinges so that the chicks can be shut in when desired. Place a bottom on it but no top. Cleats are nailed on the inside so that a cloth-covered frame will fit down on the inside of the brooder close enough to drop down over the backs of the chicks. This cloth-covered frame is just an ordinary frame made of lath or other light stuff to which an old piece of woolen blanket is tacked so that it will sag down in the middle. On top of this one places other cloths or woolen pieces, as necessary, to keep the chicks warm. One can tell, half an hour after they have been placed in the brooder, by running the hand over their backs whether they are too cold or too warm and adjust the coverings accordingly.

Oil Lamp Brooders

Oil lamp brooders, practically all of which are of the portable type, are also to be used in connection with a colony coop, brood coop or brooder house and are not "outdoor" brooders in the sense that they can be set down outside without affording other protection to the chicks, except on mild days. Then they must be brought in at night. Ordinarily, these brooders are not rated to handle more than 100 to 150 chicks per brooder, and they generally will not handle comfortably and to the best advantage all they are rated to handle. As the chicks increase in size, they outgrow the brooders and should be divided into smaller flocks for the best results.

CHAPTER VIII

These brooders, practically all of which are constructed of galvanized iron, depend upon small kerosene lamps for the heating source. The lamps must be trimmed and filled each day, although most of them have sufficient capacity to run two days, but regardless of this, one must not be careless and neglect the lamps a single day. The wick forms a crust and the tendency is to lose in the amount of heat generated unless this crust is promptly removed each day.

The earlier brooders of this type were a distinct death trap for many reasons. Generally, the heating plant or lamp was so exposed to the portion of the brooder where the chicks were that the chicks were subjected to the lamp fumes, the ventilation was bad and the chicks died by the scores. All this has been changed.

The lamp compartment is now entirely separate and away from the chick compartment. There is absolutely no chance of lamp fumes ever getting at the chicks, as a dead air space is provided which draws the heat through this drum and then out of a flue and away. The principle of the present-day portable oil lamp brooder is as near that of the mother hen as it is possible for a mechanical device to be. The heat is supplied over the chicks just as with the hen; the brooders are round and a cloth curtain extends around the whole canopy down within an inch or two of the floor. This tends to retain the heat in the chick compartment, but if the chicks become warm they will scatter out and stick their heads through the curtain, just as they do through the hen's feathers, and get fresh air. They often will roost several inches outside the cloth curtain.

For the farmer or poultryman who is raising small flocks, and by this we mean up to 1,500 chicks, we believe there is no more economical brooding device than these oil lamp brooders. They can be used right in colony coops, or unused pens in the laying house to good advantage, provided the temperature is not too low to tend to cause the chicks to chill. They are most efficient, however, for flocks less than 1,000 in size. Other systems of brooding can be found which call for less labor, but where the cost of installation is a big item, it will be best to start out with these brooders.

During the first week a temperature of 100 degrees should be maintained in the brooder. The lamp should be capable of generating more

Fig. 48—*Hollow Tile Brooder House on a Dallas County, Iowa, Farm.*

heat than this for emergencies, as in cold snaps, but that is as hot as is necessary under the hover. The temperature is gradually decreased as the chicks grow and develop allowing 96 degrees the second week, 92 degrees the third and 88 degrees the fourth week. However, it is best to follow the directions of the manufacturer, if they differ from these figures.

The application of artificial heat is generally continued until the chicks are feathered out. This will vary in different breeds. Leghorns will feather in four weeks, as a rule, if properly handled and fed, while the heavier breeds have hardly started by that time. It is seldom necessary to continue heat for Leghorns after the fourth week, unless they are hatched extremely early, but' the hover should be retained, allowing them to roost under it without heat when they seem to be comfortable. We generally retain the hovers until the chicks are old enough to teach to roost on low perches. They are more contented when this is done.

Crude Oil Brooders

There are many brooders now on the market which burn crude oil or cheap kerosene and produce a "blue flame" heat. These brooders are chiefly recommended by the manufacturers because they generate more heat and it is therefore possible to brood more chicks under the same hover. For the most part they utilize the canopy idea found in the coal burning brooder stoves and attempt to compete with these devices. They handle larger flocks than the small lamp brooders and seem to be desirable in many particulars.

Like the small lamp brooders they must be used indoors in pens provided for the chicks. They are especially desirable in colony coops. They generally come in sizes handling flocks of 100 chicks up to 500. The chief advantages given are the increased flocks brooded, automatic control of the oil, elimination of the tendency of the flame to smoke and the maintenance of an even temperature. It is claimed that these flames do not tend to "creep up" as an ordinary lamp flame does at times.

Portable Coal Hover Brooders

The coal burning brooder is another of the steps made in the progress of modern poultry methods which has made possible the present-day large scale operations. It has made possible the brooding of large flocks of chicks at a single operation, and in an economical and efficient manner. It utilizes hard coal rather than oil or kerosene because it supplies a more uniform and economical heat for the chicks.

One filling of the stove will run the colony hover for 24 hours. The regulation is automatic and the coal feeds down from the hopper into the fire box as rapidly as it is needed. It is claimed that but a few cents worth of coal is consumed per day, various estimates running from three to six cents, depending upon the size and the price of coal.

The coal burning hover is a great boon to the large flock raiser. It lightens labor, cuts costs of production and eliminates fuss and worry. It is the brooding system preeminent for the colony house system of rearing young stock and the two methods go hand in glove together.

One investigator states: "The ventilation with a coal stove brooder is ideal. Located in a large room with an abundance of fresh air, which is constantly circulating under the hover, the chicks are always supplied with pure fresh air. The metal hovers are so constructed that the heat is thrown back on the floor, making a warm zone next to the stove. Beyond this the air is cooler, and the farther away from the stove the chicks get the cooler the air becomes, so that they can be accommodated with any temperature desired, from the outside air to the extreme heat of the warm inner zone. This distribution of heat is very effective and highly desirable, especially in the early spring or during a period of bad weather. During the day the chicks will be found all over the brooder room, but at night they gather into the warmer zone about a foot from the stove and in a circle about a foot wide extending entirely around the stove. Owing to the unobstructed circulation, the chicks are supplied with an abundance of pure air while they do not suffer from lack of heat.

"Our experience for the past two years indicates that the heat can be better controlled with these coal brooders than with oil lamps. The source of heat is larger and consequently more uniform. The greatest difficulty arising from allowing the ashes to clog the fire-bed or to accumulate in the ash-pit so as to cover the drafts and kill the fire. To overcome this the fire should be shaken down twice each day and the ashes removed.

"The temperature under the hover should vary with the age of the chicks. The brood should be started at about 110 degrees F., gradually dropping this about 10 degrees each week for the first four weeks. This change in temperature must be governed by a careful study of the chicks and the outside weather conditions. If the weather is very cold or the chicks show a tendency to pile up or huddle up in groups during either the day or night, the heat should be increased."

Brooder House Methods

Brooder houses concentrate the flock of chicks under one roof and tend to make the expense and work of brooding more economical. They also make it possible for a central heating plant to not only warm the entire house to the proper temperature for the best results, but also furnish the heat for the individual hovers in each pen. This reduces labor and expense, to a degree, and makes it possible for one man to realize the most from every motion made.

Brooder houses maintaining a centralized heating plant must, of necessity, use hot water rather than hot air as the mode of heating. The plant is generally run by a hard coal stove, although soft coal may be used in them if proper pains are exerted to give the fire the extra attention demanded.

Several thousand chicks can be brooded at the same time under this system and can be hatched and developed to an age of four to six weeks before outside weather will permit them being outdoors. To the fancier and the commercial poultry farmer this offers a distinct advantage that can well be appreciated by anyone who has a grasp of conditions in the poultry world.

CHAPTER VIII

Fig. 49—Colony Brooder House With Small Run Attached for First Few Weeks.

Brooder houses, however, are not a necessity for the small flock raiser, or even for the farmer who is maintaining a flock up to a 1,000 laying hens. The farmer can more economically get along with the colony system of brooding, even though more labor is involved, because the initial cost is less and the houses can be used the entire year. The specialized brooder house can seldom be properly utilized for other stock, unless the colony coal stove brooder is the system of brooding equipment used. These stoves can be removed and stored and the house utilized for surplus cockerels or other stock.

Care of Chicks on Large Scale

It should be apparent to anyone that chicks cannot be handled on a large scale successfully unless every detail is organized in the proper manner and absolutely correct in principle. The method of brooding must be correct, the chicks must not be subjected to chilling or over-heating, and they must be closely watched at the attendant at all hours to be sure that everything is all right.

Then the methods of feeding must be correct for the particular purpose in mind. The ventilation must be correct and cleanliness must be religiously and scrupulously practiced. There never was a truer statement than that "cleanliness is next to godliness" in successfully brooding chicks. The litter must be kept clean and sweet, the accumulation of filth and droppings soon fouling it and if allowed to pile up for a time, trouble is bound to occur.

The feed given must be clean and wholesome. The drinking founts and pans must be carefully and regularly scoured and disinfected. In other words, eternal vigilance and eternal vigilance only is the price of success. Nine times in ten the troubles arising in the development of young chicks is due to the fault— the omission or the commission— of some wrongful act on the part of the attendant. The human element is at the bottom of almost every devilment arising m the brooder house today, thanks to the high state of perfection attained in our housing plans and in the manufacture of brooding equipment.

CHAPTER IX

How to Feed Poultry of All Ages

Principles of Feeding— Value of Rations— First Feeding of Baby Chicks— Feeding Baby Chicks to Feather Them Out — From Three to Eight Weeks— Two Months to Maturity— Feeding for Market— Feeding the Laying Flock— Feeding the Breeders

Feeding has been practically reduced to a science in the past twenty years. The average feeder today thinks in terms of rations, whereas he formerly thought in terms of individual grains. He has learned through the results achieved in experimental work that no single grain is a perfect ration supplying all the elements necessary to promote economical growth and healthful gain, or for any other purpose that might be in his mind.

Variety is the rule in nature and it is through a variety of grains and ingredients properly balanced and mixed with due reference to their feeding properties that the feeder secures the phenomenal results today. The 200-egg hen and the 300-egg hen are fully as much the result of proper feeding as they are the result of proper breeding. Hundreds of good hens in farm flocks today are prevented from returning their best to the farmer because they are not fed in such a way as to get the inherent ability resting in them into play. One authority on breeding high fecundity in layers has said that the problem now is to " feed out the lay already bred" in hens.

The foremost principle of feeding poultry of any age is to keep in mind the purpose you are feeding for and then to bend every effort to accomplish that purpose. That is the only thought necessary to make economical feeding possible. Many people feed aimlessly and without giving due thought to what they are about. They never stop to analyze the things they are doing, or they would discontinue many practices which they can hardly help but know are a detriment to their success in feeding. Skipping a feeding every day or two may be more convenient for the feeder, but it is not going to secure uniform results from the flock.

Fig. 50—Proper Rations and Systematic Care Produced This Uniform Flock of Pullets.

The scientist, through his examination of the ingredients and properties necessary to accomplish a given result has been able to tell us just what was necessary for us to do in order to secure those results in the most direct manner. He has then, in turn, examined all of the feeds and feed-stuffs available and found the proper proportions to use in accomplishing the results sought. In short, he has found the means of satisfying the want. There is little remaining for the busy farmer or the commercial poultryman but to confirm in his own experience the value of the formulas and rations advocated.

Some rations are better than others, but other rations may be more economical to feed, in view of the results obtained, and it is wise for the careful feeder to be ever on the lookout for improvement in the direction of lower feeding costs, as well as in the direction of results. For, in the end, the man with the lowest cost of production is the man who is going to be in better condition to meet competition and secure the maximum reward.

The first principle of profitable feeding, then, is to secure the definite result in mind as directly as possible, and the second principle is to secure the result as economically as possible.

Value of Rations

The chief value of a ration is that it tends to secure the result in mind as directly as possible, and it eliminates practically all guess-work from the feeding operations. It reduces to a simple process what might otherwise be a complicated problem calling for painstaking work in parceling out in small lots the necessary ingredients to secure the total result in mind.

There is one important thought which should always be kept in mind in regard to the feeding of certain specified rations and that is to feed the recommended ration in its entirety or feed it not at all. It is impossible to secure the larger results attainable by feeding a part of one ration and filling out with a part of another. The various rations have been formulated to supplement each other and they should always be fed in their entirety.

By this, we mean that if you adopt a mash ration recommended for winter egg laying, be sure to use the scratch grain mixture recommended with it. The two have been formulated to supplement each other and if one is used without the other, you are upsetting the balance they have been given by the blending of the grains for their feeding properties necessary for winter egg production.

Any person who expects to enter the commercial egg business, or who is anxious to secure the best returns from a side-line flock, who persists in the old haphazard way of feeding this or that grain, is either a fool or a chump with the odds in favor of the proposition that he is both. Yet hundreds of people refuse to adopt the suggestions in regard to feeding that are to be had on every hand for the mere asking, and then worry along with a non-laying flock through the winter months. They are the ones who spend good money for fake egg tonics and nostrums which are supposed to touch the hidden spring of winter egg production and bring the eggs by some magic-trick, at a dollar a bottle or can.

First Feeding of Baby Chicks

The manner in which the baby chicks are started out is going to determine, in a large measure, their future worth. One authority has said that a chick properly handled the first week is half raised, and we doubt if the truth of the matter was ever more graphically presented. Brooding the first week plays an important part, but equal to it is the manner in which you feed it.

There is no arbitrary time by the clock when you should give the chicks their first feed. Some people advise waiting as long as 72 hours after they are hatched before giving them the first feeding. While we recognize the fact that nature has provided for the first hours of a chick's life, making immediate feeding unnecessary, we also incline to the belief that nature should be the guide as to the time to start feeding. As soon as the chicks are old enough to run about and pick at things they are old enough to have their first feeding. They are not going to eat enough the first feedings to do any particular harm and they are going to get "on their feet" quicker if the first feed is proper.

Fig. 51—Young Stock Being Fed for Early Maturity—Dry Mash in Hopper Against House and Trough for Moist Mash in Foreground.

The very first thing we do is to give the chicks a good drink of sweet milk. Place it in saucers and as you take each chick out of the brooder, dip its bill in the milk. Be sure that it gets a good swallow of the milk. Then sprinkle a little commercial chick feed on clean boards or papers and try to teach them to eat. As soon as they seem to become chilly, put them back under the hover, and keep them under the hover as much as possible the first two or three days. Feed them five to seven times a day and not more than 10 minutes at a feeding.

Give them nothing to drink the first week except clean sweet milk, if at all possible. Milk will get them started better than anything else.

The secret of baby chick feeding is to feed little, feed often and feed regularly. Regularity in feeding is worth almost as much as the proper ration. And lack of regularity in feeding and in care is the big reason why so many people fail to achieve results even where the ration is proper.

Millet seed is a good feed for the first week, and we have found ordinary commercial chick food to be very good for the grain portion. This should contain as wide a variety of fine grains or cracked grains as possible. In addition, it is well to start them out on a good mash within a day or two after getting them on feed and after they have learned to feed and drink and take care of themselves. The various commercial buttermilk mashes are very good, but we prefer to feed it dry. In fact, less losses are apt to occur where all mashes are fed dry.

A number of different rations can be used for the first feeding of baby chicks, but it is best to pick out one good one and stick to it. The U. S. Department of Agriculture gives the following recommendations:

"The first feed should consist of a baked johnnycake broken up into small pieces, or hard-boiled eggs mixed with stale bread crumbs or dry oatmeal, using a sufficient amount of the cereal to make a dry, crumbly mixture. These feeds or combinations of feeds may be used with good results for a week; then gradually substitute for one or two feeds each day a mixture of equal parts of finely cracked wheat, cracked corn and pinhead oatmeal or hulled oats, to which may be added a small quantity of broken rice, millet rape seed, or charcoal, if obtainable. This mixture makes an ideal ration. If corn cannot be had, cracked kafir or rolled or hulled barley may be substituted. A commercial chick feed containing a variety of grains can be bought from most feed dealers and may be used instead of the home mixture if desired.

Cornmeal, 5 pounds; infertile eggs, 6; baking soda, 1 tablespoon. Mix with milk to make stiff batter and bake thoroughly. If infertile eggs are not available, use double quantity of baking soda and one-third pound sifted beef scraps,

"When the chicks are from 10 days to two weeks old use a mash composed of the following, to take the place of the johnnycake or bread. All ingredients are measured by weight:

Bran, 2 parts; oatmeal, 2 parts; cornmeal, 1 part; meat scrap, 10 per cent of mixture.

"This mash may be placed in a hopper, where it cannot be wasted, and left before the chicks at all times, or it may be fed as a moist, crumbly mash once each day, and the grains fed the chicks three times a day. "When the chicks are eight to 10 weeks old add 1 part of ground oats, increase the meat scrap to 20 per cent and cornmeal to 2 parts and decrease the bran to 1 part."

Keep dry wheat bran before the chicks from the first day in flat pans an inch deep. It is one of the best elements in the chick ration we have run across and you will be surprised at the amount they will eat. Also keep plenty of fresh water before them (it should be changed at every feeding), chick grit, and charcoal. The litter should be fine chaff or short cut alfalfa meal. We have found alfalfa meal the very best litter.

Feeding Baby Chicks to Feather Them Out

After the chicks have gotten on their feet, the very first object the feeder has in mind should be to feather them out. If he will feed to that end he can generally accomplish the purpose from two to several weeks sooner than will be the case where "nature is allowed to take her course."

We have found the persistent feeding of wheat bran to feather baby chicks out faster than anything we have run across. It should be kept before them dry from the day they are started out until they are practically matured. You will be surprised at the enormous quantities they will eat of it. It is also supplemented by as many elements derived from wheat as possible to induce the chicks to eat. Wheat middlings in the mash mixture and cracked wheat in the chick grain mixture all aid in bringing the feathers. It is possible to feather Leghorn chicks completely by the time they are around a month old, and it requires a little more time on the larger breeds.

From Three to Eight Weeks

By the time the chicks are three weeks old, especially in Leghorns, one should have determined for what purpose they are intended and they should be fed for that purpose. If they are to be sent to market as broilers-, they should be fed a different ration than if they are to be matured for breeders or layers. If they are to go to market, they are to be fed for

CHAPTER IX

flesh and fat, and if to be matured, they are to be fed for bone and muscle. And the man or woman who knows in detail the object sought is in a better position to realize it by making every motion count.

Where the chicks are confined to the brooder or colony house, keep a small amount of chick grain mixed in the litter to induce exercise and keep them busy. Wheat bran in the boxes should also be before them, and if one wishes to supplement it with a better mash, the following will give excellent results:

200 pounds bran

100 pounds fine oatmeal, ground oats or rolled oats

100 pounds cornmeal

75 pounds sifted beef scrap

35 pounds bone meal

25 pounds chick size charcoal

2 pounds salt

Supplement this mash with the following grain ration: 200 pounds chick size cracked corn; 300 pounds cracked wheat and 100 pounds cut oatmeal. The chicks are to have access to the dry mash at all times, and the grain mixture is given two or three times a day, just enough to keep them busy.

Green food or finely cut clover is supplied every day. Clip the green shoots off sprouted oats and this will be excellent for them. If possible let them have sweet milk to drink but don't let it sour in the pans between feedings.

Two Months to Maturity

By the time the chicks are two months old, their whole nature soon changes and everything goes to the development of frame. They seem to be light in weight and cannot be kept in good flesh. They have heavy appetites and will eat an enormous amount of feed.

The object the feeder now has in mind is to keep pace with the demands made on their systems by nature and to supply them the elements needed as fast as possible. This is best done by using every effort to stimulate their appetites by feeding little and feeding often and by adding a moist mash to the ration to encourage them eating more than they otherwise would.

Fig. 52—Five-months-old pullet developed by proper feeding. Has just, laid" her first egg.

The simplest and best mash to use for this purpose is one composed of equal parts, wheat bran, corn meal and ground oats or oatmeal, thoroughly mixed, to which is added at least two parts of alfalfa meal, all moistened until crumbly but not wet or sloppy, with sweet milk. Salt the mixture to taste. Feed this twice a day, in the middle of the forenoon and afternoon, as a supplement to the other feeding done. It does not take the place of the mash mentioned above, it merely supplements it. Be regular in your feeding time and note the great gains made in development.

Success at this stage of the chicks ' development rests in feeding every bit the chicks can be made to eat, but not feeding so much that they lose their appetite? and get "off feed." This can best be regulated by not feeding too much of the moist mash mentioned. If you leave them slightly hungry they will, go back to the litter or the dry mash hoppers and will keep right on working. That is the secret back of proper feeding.

After the chicks are two months of age you can commence to feed them whole oats. For the first week feed the oats at noon after they have been soaked in water since morning. After a week they can be fed dry, without any disastrous results. We believe whole oats, in fact, oats in any form, to be one of the most valuable developing foods for chicks that could be recommended. Feed all they will eat in pans at noon.

Feeding for Market

Where the chicks are intended for broilers for market, slightly different methods should be followed. They are handled the first three weeks as recommended above after which they are fed to develop flesh and fat. Success in market feeding comes through the old secret of feeding little and feeding often and in being regular to the dot at each feeding period. The slightest deviation may throw the chicks off and cause you to lose some of the advantages gained.

If all the feed can be moistened with milk, so much the better. Of course the grain fed morning and night is not to be moistened, nor the dry wheat bran which is before them all the time. They are not permitted to have dry mash because they can be induced to eat more of the moistened mash, if it is properly handled. Grit and water should also be before them all the time.

The mash, which consists of equal parts wheat bran, cornmeal and ground oats with as much alfalfa meal as they can be induced to eat, all moistened with sweet milk and fed in clean pans, is gradually changed after they are four weeks old, the bran being changed to middlings until one-sixth of the whole mixture is composed of it, and after the sixth week the corn meal is gradually increased. Salt the moist mash to taste. Allow the chicks to eat for 10 or 15 minutes and then remove the mash pans from the pens until the next feeding, scattering a handful of grain in the litter to set them to work. Chicks intended for broilers should be kept confined to the colony coop or brooder pen. Feed five times per day, giving the grain mixture in the morning and cracked corn at night and the moist mash at 10 o'clock, noon and 3 o'clock.

Chicks fed regularly on this ration will attain a weight of two pounds at the age of eight weeks for the heavier breeds and a pound and one-half to two pounds for Leghorn cockerels in the same time. They are then ready for the broiler market.

Feeding the Laying Flock

We now come to a consideration of the question of greatest interest to the most people. What shall I feed my layers to secure the best egg yield? is a common question asked on every hand. There is no one best ration, but there are a number of good rations which every farmer should be able to supply his hens. Feeding is not the result of mysterious power or ability so much as it is the result of good, common sense in supplying the hens with the elements necessary to make a good egg yield possible.

Many people kick on the fact that their hens are eating a great deal and they think they are "saving" money by cutting down the amount fed. A more foolish idea was never held than that. The more a hen eats the better the chance that she is a good layer. The heavy laying hen will require considerably more feed than an average layer or one that is not laying at all. Give the hens liberal feeding of the sort of ration they ought to have. They can't eat too much of the right sort of feeds.

Six good rations have been worked out at the government poultry farm in Maryland, which are recommended by the U. S. Department of Agriculture for laying flocks. They are:

Ration No. 1

Mash
16 pounds corn meal
6 1/4 pounds meat scrap
1 pound bran
1 pound middlings

Scratch Mixture
1 pound cracked corn
1 pound wheat
1 pound oats

Ration No. 2

2 pounds corn or barley meal
1 pound bran
1 pound middlings
1 pound meat or fish scraps

2 pounds cracked corn
1 pounds oats
1 pound wheat or barley

Ration No. 3

3 pounds corn meal
1 pound meat scrap

2 pounds cracked corn
1 pound oats

Ration No. 4

9 pounds corn meal
5 pounds middlings
4 pounds bran
2 pounds cottonseed or gluten meal
2 pounds meat scrap
2 per cent bone meal

2 pounds cracked corn
1 pound wheat
1 pound oats
1 pound barley

Ration No. 5

1 pound corn meal
1 pound bran
¾ pound meat scrap
1 pound middlings
1 pound ground oats

2 pounds cracked corn
1 pound wheat
1 pound oats
1 pound barley

CHAPTER IX

Ration No. 6

3 pounds corn meal
1 pound bran
1 pound middlings
1/2 pound meat scrap
Feed with table scraps
or cooked vegetables

2 pounds cracked corn
1 pound wheat
1 pound oats

The Department gives these recommendations as to feeding: "The scratch mixture should be fed twice daily, preferably in deep litter from 3 to 5 inches deep on the floor of the henhouse. Feed about one-third of the mixture in the morning and two-thirds in the afternoon. In the morning give only what the fowls will eat up within half an hour and at night enough to fully satisfy them. Feed a mash either as a dry or moist feed in addition to the scratch grains. The dry mash is the more common method; it should be kept in a hopper before the fowls constantly. A moist (not sloppy) mash gives very good results when used by a careful feeder. It should be fed only once a day, preferably in the morning or at noon, and only as much should be fed as the fowls will clean up in from 15 to 30 minutes. A moist mash is very useful to use up table scraps and cooked vegetables and is greatly improved if mixed with milk. The quantity of meat scrap used in the mash can be reduced in proportion to the garbage and milk used . . .

"The feeder must use his own judgment in deciding how much grain to give the hens, as the amount of feed which they will eat varies with different pens and at different seasons of the year. They will eat more feed in the spring while laying heavily than in the summer and fall when laying fewer eggs. A fair general estimate is to feed about 1 quart of scratch grains and an equal weight of mash (about 1 1/2 quarts) daily to 13 hens of the general purpose breeds, such as the Plymouth

Rocks, Rhode Island Reds, or Wyandottes, or to 16 hens of the smaller or egg breeds. This would be about 7 1/2 pounds each of scratch grains and of mash daily to 100 Leghorns and about 9 1/2 pounds each to 100 general purpose fowls. If hens have free range or large yards containing green food a general purpose hen will eat about 75 pounds of feed in a year and a Leghorn will eat about 55 pounds, in addition to the green stuff consumed."

The following ration is recommended in high terms by an Eastern commercial egg farmer who has been raising Leghorns and selling market eggs on a large scale for many years. The grain mixture consists in summer of half corn and half wheat and in winter of two-thirds of corn and one-third wheat. In addition, the hens have all the sprouted oats they will eat at one feeding in winter. In summer soaked oats is fed instead of sprouted oats in order to save time. It is unnecessary to sprout oats then because the hens have range.

The mash ration fed in connection with the grain, is as follows:

2 parts bran
2 parts middlings
2 parts ground oats, oat meal or rolled oats
1 part gluten meal
½ part oil meal
2 parts corn meal
1 part fish scraps
¾ part best beef scraps
½ part chick charcoal
½ pound salt to every 100 pounds above.

The above mash is kept before the hens all the time with the exception of when they are molting. "We have fed all kinds of recipes," says this poultryman, "but this is the one we have worked out ourselves and it is giving us good satisfaction. Some mashes contain more protein than this, and others less, but with the amount of other grains fed in connection with this mash we get a very nicely balanced ration."

Another commercial poultryman uses this ration:

Dry Mash	*Scratch Feed*
50 pounds bran	30 pounds cracked corn
10 pounds ground corn	30 pounds feed wheat
5 pounds cut clover	30 pounds clipped oats
10 pounds meat crisps	3 1/3 pounds kaffir corn
26 ounces salt	3 1/3 pounds sunflower seed

10 pounds shorts

5 pounds ground oats

3 pounds cut alfalfa

10 pounds flax-seed

3 1/3 pounds buckwheat

The ration used at the New Jersey Experiment Station is more uniform in the amount of the individual ingredients used and is as follows:

Mash

100 pounds wheat bran

100 pounds corn meal

100 pounds ground oats

100 pounds meat scraps

Grain

100 pounds cracked corn

100 pounds wheat

100 pounds oats

The famous Cornell Laying Ration, a little more complicated, however, is as follows:

Mash

60 pounds cornmeal

60 pounds middlings

50 pounds meat scraps

30 pounds bran

10 pounds oil meal

10 pounds alfalfa meal

1 pound salt

Grain

3 parts wheat

2 parts corn

1 part oats

This wide choice of a laying ration may be confusing to some people but we offer the choice simply because it often happens that certain ingredients in a ration cannot easily or economically be procured by people living in given localities. Instead of adopting the common plan of omitting that ingredient from the ration, as most people do where they have only one formula at hand, we consider it better to make it possible for one in such circumstances to adopt another entire ration better fitting his needs and possibilities, as offering the most in ultimate satisfaction.

Fig. 53—The Importance of Plenty of Fresh Water for Fowls of All Ages Must Not Be Overlooked.

There is no reason why every farm flock should not be managed under one of the above rations. They will all achieve the purpose in mind; namely, make the production of eggs possible, if carefully followed. Of all the rations recommended, we feel that the New Jersey ration will find the greatest favor among farmers because of the ease with which it can be mixed, requiring equal parts of all ingredients used in both the grain and mash mixtures. It is also composed of ingredients commonly found or obtainable on all farms with the exception of meat scraps, and they must be purchased for any ration and if one desires to secure the maximum performance from the laying flock. Many people substitute tankage for the meat scrap element in laying rations and report that they are receiving satisfactory results.

Next in importance we would place Ration No. 3 recommended by the Department of Agriculture. It is extremely simple in formula and should be easily mixed on any farm; it is doubtful, however, if it will be as entirely satisfactory as the New Jersey rations. In fact, there is nothing impractical in any of the rations recommended. They all come from authoritative sources and are based upon hard-headed and practical experience.

In addition, there are two important considerations to keep in mind in feeding laying hens. First, the supply of fresh water must be constant at all times, particularly in cold weather. Hens denied an abundance of water will not lay at their full capacity. The second point is that all rations must be supplemented by liberal feedings of sprouted oats at noon, or other green food.

Feeding the Breeders

The point of foremost consideration in feeding the breeding flock is to secure fertile eggs. While you wish a goodly supply of eggs for hatching purposes that is not the point of first consideration, for an infertile egg is worthless and it is better to have none at all than one that will not produce a good, strong chick. Your idea, then, is to feed for fertility, if feeding has any effect upon fertility.

In other words, every effort at artificial stimulation for egg production must be eliminated when handling the breeding flock. Not that the feeding of heavy laying rations is especially conducive to weak constitutional vigor in the hens as layers, but because any stimulation on the reproductive organs has a very marked effect upon the fertility and hatchability of the eggs laid.

First and foremost, it is wise to cut out all meat elements in the ration. If these are from fresh lean meat or composed entirely of lean meat no ill effects are likely to occur, but we have no means of knowing whether this is true. When in doubt over an element of the ration for the breeders, cut out that element.

The feeding of liberal quantities of wheat bran and sprouted oats in the rations will entirely replace the meat scraps, tankage or green cut bone that you are in the habit of feeding the laying flock, and it will not have a disastrous effect upon the fertility of the eggs.

As much bulky food as the hens can be induced to eat should be fed as this tends to increase fertility and hatchability of eggs— such feeds as wheat bran, alfalfa meal, sprouted oats, cut clover, etc.

A good ration for breeders is equal parts wheat, cracked corn and oats for the scratch grain and for the mash equal parts bran, ground oats, cornmeal and one-half the mixture alfalfa meal, supplemented by sprouted oats at noon. Also plenty of water, grit, shell and charcoal.

CHAPTER X

Developing the Young Stock Properly

Importance of Systematic Care— Value and Kinds of Range — Rations and Methods

We have already made the remark that regularity in the feeding and care of the young stock is fully as important as the housing methods followed and the rations fed. We cannot state this conclusion too forcibly. Of course it is, in a certain sense, an over-emphasis but unless it is given due weight and consideration by the farmer or poultryman, it is not an over-emphasis.

We all know the wonderful results that come from regularity in our own lives. If we go to bed at a certain hour each evening, arise at a certain hour, eat wholesome food and indulge in exercise or labor regularly a certain number of hours each day, we soon find our regular habits making it possible for us not only to maintain our own but to gain weight. Every young man who came under military training will testify to the fact that he gained weight and strength while in the service, unless disease or sickness overtook him, and if he will analyze the conditions there seems to be only two outstanding facts responsible for the benefits he derived: regular habits and systematic work or exercise. The food was but slightly different from what he had been accustomed to in civilian life, especially if he came from the farm. It was the regular hours and the systematic work that made the great difference in his physical make-up.

The same consideration holds true in the proper development of the young stock. Regularity in feeding and care, having every detail of these absolutely correct, will do more to insure steady development than any ration that can be fed. That is to say that no matter how good the ration may be, if regular and systematic attention is lacking, the gains deserved from the ration will not be obtained.

There should be a regular time for every duty in connection with the care of the poultry and there is no reason why that time should be al-

Fig. 54—Colony Houses With Good Range, Proper Feeding and Regular Care Develop Young Stock at the Least Coat.

lowed to vary one minute in time from day to day. If such a schedule is followed from the time the baby chicks are given their first feeding until they are matured, you will bring the young pullets forward without a single hitch, they will develop rapidly into the sort of pullets necessary for high egg records and the cost of their production will generally be from one-third to one-half less than that obtaining where they are given indifferent and haphazard attention.

If there is one outstanding detail noticeable in visiting the farms and plants of those farmers and poultrymen who are making the best successes it is that every detail is given proper attention and that everything is done on an absolute schedule, nothing being allowed to upset or delay the work of any part of the day. And that is what was meant when it was written that "eternal vigilance is the price of success."

Any man, woman or child has sufficient ability to make a success of poultry production provided they have the will power to do the right thing as common sense reveals it to them at the right time. If one has a tendency to be careless, to put things off, to slide out of doing a disagreeable task as long as possible, then there is slight chance that they will succeed in poultry production.

The hardest job in the whole poultry yard is to be able to develop a crop of young pullets properly each season to go into the laying houses.

Many a man who can feed and handle the layers successfully falls down on this one point and unless one can make good on it, poultry keeping will not prove profitable. For one cannot stay in the business unless one can bring on a new crop of pullets year after year to take the place of those who have served their period of usefulness.

And regularity— bringing the young pullets forward with a rush from the day they are hatched and without a break— is the secret of economical and unerring pullet production. Just keep that in mind as one of the outstanding "secrets" of successful poultry work.

Value and Kinds of Range

The most economical way in which to handle young stock is to afford them every advantage on range. This means that the colony system or some adaptation of it will be necessary. We have already indicated several types of desirable colony coops and how to construct them— types practical and desirable for general farm use.

The value of range for the young stock cannot be overestimated. It not only makes for economy in the feeding, but it promotes the most rapid growth and develops stock strong in constitutional vigor and stamina. And strong, sturdy, upstanding fowls are necessary in order to stand up under the strain of heavy egg production.

Fowls developed on good range under the colony house system can be developed at a much more economical figure than under any other method. Tests at one experiment station during the peak of high prices brought out the fact that range-raised Leghorn pullets could be matured for an average cost slightly in excess of 38 cents each. Under wise management and proper conditions, this figure should be lowered several cents at the present time.

There are various kinds of range available to the farmer for his young stock. The logical place to raise young stock is generally in the farm orchard. There they will have the advantage of shade and will not be molested by other farm work. And the advantage of making the land yield a double production is also had. Chickens will not injure the productiveness of an orchard as many other farm animals will, but stand to improve that production not only by the increased fertility given the soil through their droppings but because they are the natural enemies of the enemies of the orchard such as bugs, worms and slugs.

The orchard has the further advantage of generally being close to the house where regular and prompt care and feeding will be possible. This is a point that should not be overlooked for in bad weather the tendency to be irregular in feeding and care is more pronounced if the colony coops are far removed from the main buildings.

Fig. 55—An Economical Roosting Coop for Young Stock on Range. The Ventilation Is Perfect in This Coop.

The next most desirable range for the young stock is in growing corn field. This is perhaps the most desirable place of all for the young stock were it not for the fact that the corn fields are generally some distance from the main buildings and the running back and forth to take care of the stock consumes more time, especially during the busy season. However, where the details are correctly organized and the hopper system of feeding is followed, many farmers are able to make one visit per day suffice. Of course, it is necessary to make the rounds at night and see that everything is going all right in order to anticipate and remedy trouble before it has a chance to make inroads on the young flock.

The best method is to string the colony houses along the fence row and facing the corn field. Allow plenty of space between the coops and the chicks will learn which coop is their own and will not be so likely to flock into one coop. They will range through the corn field, where the growing corn provides shade and will harvest a large crop of bugs and worms, which will be highly desirable and cut down the amount of feed necessary. The cover provided by the corn will tend to protect and shield them from hawks.

CHAPTER X

Rations and Methods

While a number of good rations have been presented in the Chapter on Feeding, constant experience will soon reveal to you the ration best suited for your needs. While the rations play a tremendous part in the proper development of young stock and must not be minimized, we want to lay particular stress at this time upon the methods of care given the young chicks.

One poultryman said to me not long ago: "There are millions of chicks lost every year that should with the proper sort of care have lived and produced a profit. When you consider what it means from a money standpoint for every chick that is lost, the amount staggers you. I figure that a chick coming from even ordinary stock that dies represents a loss to me in money of at least 50 cents."

The greatest loss in chicks unquestionably comes from overcrowding and the evils attendant thereon. Overcrowding results in dead and stunted chicks and it is the inevitable mistake made by the beginner. It takes some people several years to learn that it is not numbers that counts for the most profit in the poultry business but carefully developed and properly handled individuals. As soon as one loses sight of the importance of the individual and commences to think in terms of numbers, unless he has the solid rock of practical experience behind him, then he is inviting trouble.

Every colony house should be made to support only the number of chicks it can comfortably handle. If there is any doubt as to whether they are overcrowded or not the best plan is to reduce the number of chicks in order to be sure. It will make money for you in the long run.

Fig. 56—A Colony Coop in the Orchard is an Ideal Place to mature young stock.

Constant visits must be made to the colony coops during the growing season in order to be sure that the chicks are coming along all right. One point which must be kept in mind is to prevent overheating or chilling, as the case may be. The square corners of the coops should be rounded out every day with litter in order to make it impossible for the chicks to pile up and smother each other. Those that do not die as a result of this piling up are very apt to lose their feathers through sweating, and this is the first step towards a stunted chick.

Many poultrymen use all kinds of devices to prevent the chicks getting into the corners and piling up. If there are any nest boxes in the colony coops they must be covered up so the chicks cannot get into them and pile up. Pieces of lumber can be nailed together in such a way as to round out the corners and get away from this evil. It is one of the sure sources of losses in growing stock if the detail is not taken care of and it comes to the veteran as well as the beginner.

Keep the ventilating devices on the colony coops in working order during the summer. It should be possible to secure fresh air from any di-

CHAPTER X

rection in the colony coops. This is highly important for the continual and uninterrupted development of the young stock during hot weather.

In other words, the farmer or poultryman must keep a constant eye on the young stock and see that they are given every advantage possible to promote rapid and economical growth. The droppings must be cleaned up regularly and the houses sprayed with disinfectants. The chicks must be kept comfortable at all times and be supplied with a good ration regularly fed. That is about all that is necessary. It is in the details that the rub comes.

CHAPTER XI

Culling Farm Poultry for Any Purpose

Culling Continually Practiced— Purpose of Culling— Culling Young Stock— Fall Culling of Pullets— Gulling the Layers— External Characteristics op Good Layers

Culling is not a seasonal work in the poultry yard as many people are likely to assume from the annual fall culling demonstrations staged by county agents and extension workers. It is a process that should be going on all the time if the maximum results are to be expected from the fowls, regardless of their age.

Nature has a habit of penalizing the poultryman and carrying on a culling work all her own, if he fails to do the proper things at the right time. And Nature is much more severe in her methods than is necessary, hence it is wise to pay the voluntary tax of doing the work at the right time before Nature assesses the involuntary tax and disease breaks out in the flock.

It is wise to start on the first day and destroy all weaklings, all chicks with crooked toes, and to keep, up a ruthless program of culling until the fowls are finally disposed of. It increases the individual returns won from each member of the flock and it reduces the chance of loss through outbreaks of disease. Disease generally finds its surest stepping stone to the rest of the flock through the weaklings and drones.

From an economic standpoint the continual plan of culling is also desirable because it cuts the expense of feeding and housing to a minimum by saving that consumed by those individuals which are not returning, and will not return, any income.

Fig. 57—High-producing Leghorns, having record of 288 and 269 eggs, respectively, showing bodily capacity and long backs necessary in goodlayers.

While this continual process of culling is going on, through the simple plan of watching the fowls and eliminating the undesirables as fast as noted, there are also times when it is profitable to go through the whole flock and subject it to rigid culling tests. And certain seasons are more advantageous for this work than others.

Purposes of Culling

The primary purpose of culling is to discover the drones in the flock, or those unlikely to earn a profit, as quickly as possible. The culls create a tiny leak in the poultry business dyke which sooner or later will undermine and destroy the whole structure as a business unit unless these heroic measures are adopted in self-protection.

Culling is not an intricate or highly specialized work. Any person of average intelligence can learn the rudiments of the work in a few hours and cull to a fair percentage of accuracy. With practice comes confidence and the knowledge that will soon make anyone as expert a culler as the highly paid experts who devote most of their time at certain seasons of the year to this work.

We do not always cull to the same end, and the farmer should keep in mind at all times what he is trying to do when he commences to cull.

CHAPTER XI

The fancier will term all fowls that do not measure up to his individual requirements, as he interprets the Standard of Perfection, culls. Oftentimes the fancier will throw out the fowl having the most desirable utility or egg-laying ability. In fact, all of the English Leghorns, without exception, would be culls under the fancier's way of looking at things.

To the farmer desiring high egg-laying ability, however, the exact reverse would probably be true. To him the fine looking birds might be considered as culls. This all goes to prove that any fowl which does not measure up to the particular requirements we have in mind, are culls, and they do not necessarily mean stunted, runty, poorly-developed fowls. A stalk of corn in a flower bed is a "weed" and it is on the same general theory that poultry culling is done.

It is necessary to know at all times the goal in mind and to work untiringly to that end. Then and then only will culling play the important part in your work that it should.

Culling Young Stock

Culling young stock, and by that we mean the stock which has not reached maturity, is reduced to a few simple rules easily understood by all and easily applied.

The very first standard by which the growing stock can be culled is by their general development as compared with other individuals in the flock. Those who lag behind and seem to be making no progress should be taken out of the flock, penned up and fattened, if possible, and sent to market. All chicks that do not develop uniformly with the average in the flock should be penned up and either fattened or specially fed so that they can have a chance to make up the lost ground, if it seems that there is a chance for them growing into serviceable individuals.

A common case is where some of the chicks seem unable to develop and grow feathers along with the rest of the flock. These eases, as soon as they are noted, should be taken in hand, rather than allowing them to run loose all summer without making any further progress. Sometimes it is possible to get the feathers started by penning them up and feeding liberally on wheat bran, wheat middlings and cracked wheat. If you do not note any progress in two or three weeks it is best to use other methods in disposing of them, as the chances are that they will never develop feathers properly. But a great number of these- -cases can be corrected if taken in hand soon enough.

There is always a number of deformed or odd chicks in almost every flock of youngsters. The first step in culling is to weed out these chicks and either kill them or dispose of them in some manner. They are of no economic advantage and stand a chance of being a serious detriment to the success of the flock.

The next step to keep in mind is to separate the young cockerels from the flock as soon as they can be distinguished, place them in a separate pen and feed them a fattening ration as outlined in the chapter on feeding so that they can be gotten to market with the least possible delay. The huskiest and most promising of these young cockerels may be desired for breeding purposes, in which event they should be placed in a still different pen and fed to develop strong, sturdy muscular frames.

The sooner this is done the greater the profit from those that go to market and the better the chance for the pullets retained in the original flock. Every day of delay in getting the culls to market takes just that much profit out of the pocket of the poultryman and adds that much to the cost of the pullets matured. We might say in this connection that the correct way to figure the net cost of the pullets matured in each lot is to deduct from the gross cost the returns received from the marketing of the cockerels weeded out.

In culling young stock, then, adopt these general plans: First, cull out the undesirables, the weaklings, the runts and stunted chicks. Second, cull the cockerels as rapidly as possible in order that the maximum return may be secured from them for broiler purposes.

Fall Culling of Pullets

The best time for a general culling of the young pullets is in the fall just before they are taken in from the range and placed in the laying houses. Most people delay this work until the frosty nights come along in October, but many farmers in the Middle West who have given the matter attention state that it is better to get the pullets in by the middle of September. Whatever the exact time of making the move, to be determined largely by the locality and the season, the whole flock should be carefully gone over and the undesirables culled out.

CHAPTER XI

The first consideration that will naturally be considered as the individual fowls are taken up and examined will be the weight and development they have attained. Those seeming to be behind the rest in size and flesh will naturally be separated from the main flock. They will not commence to lay as a rule as soon as the rest and should be placed to themselves where they can be given a special feeding in an effort to push their development before cold weather really sets in.

It is really regrettable that little work has been done by the investigators in learning how to cull pullets at the start of the laying season in order to determine which ones are going to be the best layers. Practically everything that has been done has been done along the line of determining the layer at the end of the first year, or at least after the flock has been producing eggs for several months. It stands to reason that the most valuable time at which to have a clear index to the ability of the pullets to go into the flock would be at the start of the season before the drones have had an opportunity to consume their portion of the ration and the attendant's time, during which period they are contributing nothing towards the income.

There are some general characteristics, however, by which the culler can be guided in the early fall work which will serve to keep the amount of cull pullets down to a minimum. One or two investigators have commenced to devote attention to this subject. We quote from a bulletin recently issued by the Michigan Agricultural College:

"Egg type in poultry is more reliably indicated by the head than any other single part of the body. The head reveals health, constitutional vigor, age, refinement, coarseness, and masculinity. Lady Activity (record 253 eggs in 365 days) was selected as the record hen in the college flock in 1916 just as she began to lay, selection being based chiefly on refinement of head. Care and judgment must be exercised, however, or refinement of head will lead to the selection of individuals that are not sufficiently robust to stand up under the continuous strain of heavy egg production. Small heads and extreme fineness of features generally indicate a propensity for broodiness.

"Early maturity also is correlated with heavy egg production. The pullet that feathers earliest on the back has, in nearly every case, made the highest yearly records. Early feathering over the back is an indication of both early maturity and constitutional vigor. Chicks always feather in the following definite order: wings, tail, neck, breast, fluff and back. Chicks of the heavy breeds, should be feathered over the back at seven weeks of age. Leghorns or lighter breeds, a week earlier. Preference should also be given to close, tight feathers, along with early feathering."

Earlier maturity is one of the surest tests we now have as to the probable value as layers of the pullets. It is almost a sure indication that the pullet which matures during a period ranging from five to seven months, depending upon the breed, is going to be the best layer. On the other hand, those that linger for several weeks seemingly making no progress are not so likely to develop into the best producers.

Fig. 58—Showing Desirable Head on Good Layer.

This, however, must be tempered by the time when the chicks were hatched and due reference given to the possibility of the young pullets undergoing a fall molt. If Leghorn pullets, for instance, are hatched in February or March they will nearly always commence to lay in midsummer and then undergo a molt during the early fall along with the other hens. This causes them to stop laying and they seldom get back to producing eggs before the middle of the winter. This means that the poultryman is going to have to know the exact time in which to hatch his pullets if he wants to mature them at a time so that there is slight danger of them going through this annoying molt. April hatched Leghorn pullets seldom, if ever, go through this molt and generally go a year and a half before molting. The same thing applies to pullets of the larger breeds, if hatched too soon.

All of the tests applied to hens that have been laying are not of value in culling the pullets. As a rule these tests are of slight value with the exception of the pelvic bone tests to indicate probable capacity. The pigmentation tests or tests by noting the presence or absence of the yellow coloring matter, are of no value whatever in testing out pullets that have not yet commenced to lay.

CHAPTER XI

Culling the Layers

What is the good type and how can we pick out the layers in our flock? The characteristics of good layers are external as well as internal—so much so that one can oftentimes spot the good layer on sight without having to handle the birds. The first thing one does when looking at a herd of dairy cattle is to look at the "business end" of the animals, if speculating on whether or not they are good producers. Dairy cows are judged largely for their capacity or heavy milk flow. The same holds true in the case of the heavy-laying hen. She must have proper vent capacity just as the dairy animal must have proper udder development for heavy production.

Fig. 59—The Small, Snaky Head on Undesirable Layers.

Wide depth and capacity in the abdominal region is a strong indication of the heavy layer in the case of hens. She conforms, in a general way, to the outline found in the high-producing animal. Rather than being a fowl of curves, she is a fowl of triangles. If a hen lacks appearance of great capacity or depth of keel before one takes her in hand to examine, the chances are very strong against her being a good layer. The stunted hen, the poorly matured pullet, and the nonproducer always give strong indications lacking in this particular before they are ever examined in detail.

On the other hand, hens sloppy in appearance and shape seldom prove to be good layers. This does not necessarily mean the hen that is ragged in feathers, but with the hen having a baggy vent it is generally true. Abdominal capacity is the first general characteristic to examine in culling the flock.

Looseness and pliability of the skin is a better indication of the healthy layer when found around the vent, than a thick, tough skin. The vent should be moist rather than dry, and a slight pressure should evidence this in the hen that is a good layer.

The head points are another very good indication of the laying ability of your hens. The hen with a pale, dry, waxy comb and wattles, with thin face, pale beak, eye rings and ear lobes, with a bright round eye, is generally rated as a good layer. On the other hand, the poor layer ordinarily shows small, hard, dry combs and wattles, with a fat face, yellow beak, eye rings and ear lobe's; the ear lobes are often wrinkled, and she has a pale, snaky eye. The hen with the small, snaky head, in general, or the full, beefy neck, should be discarded as undesirable.

The pigmentation test is another very good external test to use in culling the flock. We used to think that the hens with the nice, bright shanks and yellow beaks were the most desirable to keep and the others were gathered up and sent off to market. Investigations the past few years have demonstrated the fact that the hen with the yellow rings and beak is, in fact, a mediocre layer and not paying for her board. This is due to the fact that the secretion of the yellow pigment in the shanks, big circles around the eyes and skin has a direct relation to the egg-laying ability of the hen. Nature secretes the yellow pigment in the places mentioned for a definite purpose, and as the hen lays her clutch of eggs this secretion is drawn upon for coloring matter in the yolks, and at the height of the laying season it is consumed more rapidly than it is secreted. This results in the distinct bleaching of the birds so that at the end of the laying season the shanks of the heavy layer will, in fact, be practically white in color. The poor layer, not drawing upon the secretions of pigment, retains the natural bright luster in her shanks and the other points of secretion and is naturally the most "healthy" looking hen in the flock.

Investigations in regard to the pigmentation test have developed to such a point that before long the experiment stations will be prepared to announce definitely the exact number of days of laying required to consume the pigment stored in any one part of the body of the fowl. When this matter is finally determined definitely it will be possible for the farmer to select a hen and tell at once just how many eggs she has laid that year. In the meantime the indications obviously offered by the pigmentation test should not be overlooked, because they are one of the surest indexes the farmer can use in drafting the layers.

Another indication of the good layer is that of temperament. One can seldom fail on this test if one has the time and desire to watch the hens closely. The good layer is always a hustler and of a nervous temperament. There is no indication of sluggishness in her make-up. She is ever busy, has a good appetite, and continually on the move. On the other hand, the poor layer is the sort of hen you find on the roost until noon, or standing on the sunny side of a building in spring, or in some shady spot during the hot days of summer. At times she appears to have no appetite at all. She is baggy, slovenly in appearance, and has nothing of the nervous temperament found in the busy, alert hen. Discard the lazy hen, for there is nothing to lose in sending her off to market.

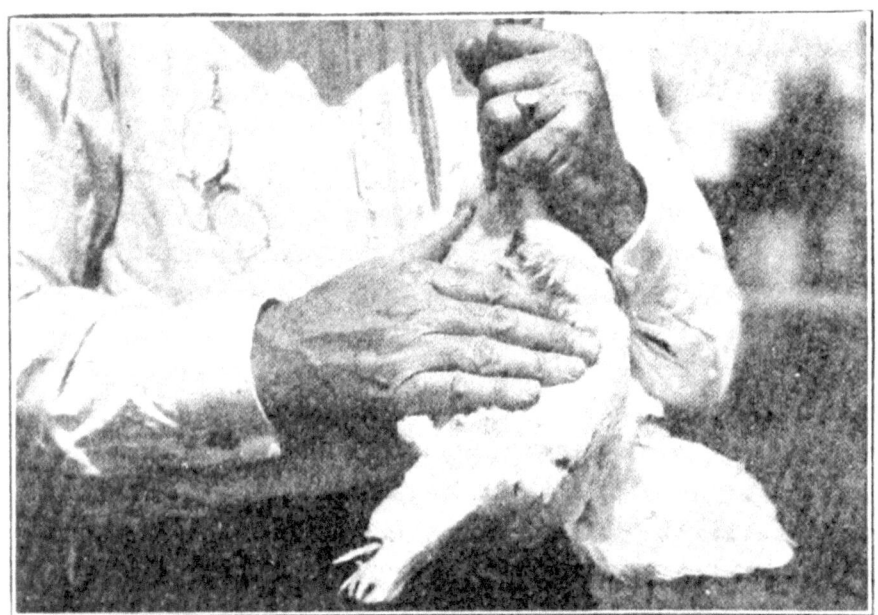

Fig. 60—Showing Desirable Abdominal Capacity for a Heavy Layer

The molting period is the best time in which to cull the laying hens, for the reason that it has a very strong influence upon the laying record of each individual. We used to think that the early molters were the heavy layers for the reason that they would be through molting in time to resume laying in the fall. This idea, however, has been proved largely erroneous. The poor layer always starts to molt while stopping production through the fall months, and very seldom laying until the natural period returns in the spring. The heavy layer, on the other hand, if she molts at all, goes through very slow molt during the fall, laying right up until cold weather in many cases, sometimes being pushed to grow a new coat of feathers before severe weather sets in. This hen is manifestly the most profitable to the farmer, because she keeps up her production throughout the late summer and early fall, not only paying her way, but giving the farmer the advantage of the higher prices obtained for her eggs in the early fall months. The cold weather naturally hastens the production of a new coat of feathers, and you will find the late molter back to laying from six weeks to two months in many cases. All hens that are not molting in July, August, and in some instances, September, should be examined with a great deal of care. The hens molting in the first two months can be safely discarded as unprofitable.

Hens that are well bleached, that have the proper head points, with good color and loose, pliable skin around the vent, are, as a general rule, to be selected as the hens to be retained in the laying flock. All others should be discarded as unprofitable, and sent to market.

External Characteristics of Good Layers

It is in the examination of the laying hens individually that the greatest degree of success comes in culling the flock, because it renders possible a careful and minute examination of each section of the hens, which is impossible where only general type characteristics are considered.

Culling is down to the point now where no one need fear for results after a careful individual examination has been made. It is now possible to tell almost to the egg laid, just what each hen is doing.

In the previous section we mentioned briefly the fact that the pigmentation test is one of the surest indications of the sort of layers you are examining. The word "pigmentation" refers to the yellow coloring matter found in the different sections of the body, which indicates the storage of fat subsequently going into the making of egg-yolks as the hen commences to lay. Inasmuch as the average hen seems to produce eggs faster than she can secure the necessary elements from the rations consumed, this stored-up fat is drawn upon and quickly absorbed in order to keep up egg production. This process results in the partial bleaching of the color of the hen as laying progresses, and as the fat is taken out. When we refer to the "pigmentation" test, then, we refer to the indications present of yellow pigment denoting fat.

Tests among the experiment stations have progressed so far in the direction of the pigmentation test that it is now possible to announce definitely how many eggs are required to "lay out" the yellow coloring matter in any given section of the body. Anyone who appreciates the value of culling at all can readily appreciate what a tremendous value this information has for every poultry keeper who seriously uses it.

In taking up a layer to cull under the pigmentation test, the first section to examine is the vent, or the abdominal region. We have already mentioned the general characteristics of the vent of a good potential layer, to be used in case the hens or pullets have not yet commenced to lay. It must be understood that the pigmentation test cannot be used on pullets that have not yet entered seriously upon their first laying season.

The vent is the first section to change as soon as the hen or pullet commences to lay, and it changes very rapidly with egg production, so that a white vent or a pink vent denotes that the hen is then laying, while a yellow vent is an absolute indication that the hen has not been laying.

The eye rings and the ear lobes are the next sections to be influenced under the pigmentation test. By the eye ring we mean the inner edge of the eyelid. It bleaches out a little more slowly than the vent, and the ear lobes of fowls having white ear lobes, such as Leghorns, bleach out a little slower than the eye ring, so that white ear lobes indicate a greater period of laying than where merely the vent or eye ring are bleached. The next section to bleach is the beak. The pigment leaves the beak at the base and gradually works out to the end of the upper 'beak. The lower beak bleaches faster than the upper. There is a white point on the beak present even before laying commences and it should not be confused with the other pigment. A thoroughly bleached beak indicates that the fowl has been laying for from four to six weeks.

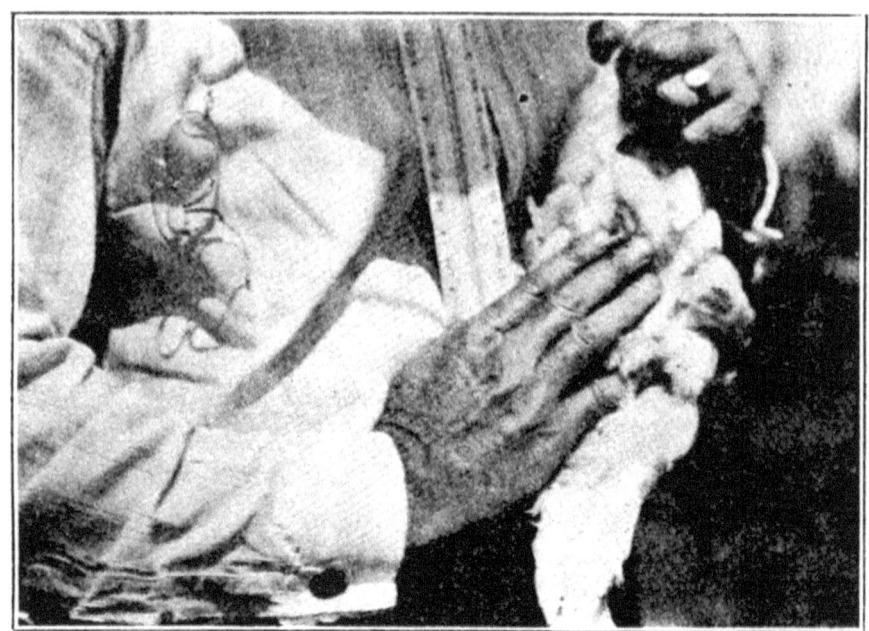

Fig. 61—Pubic Bone Test—a "Three-Finger" Hen Having Fairly High Productive Capacity.

The shanks are the last section of the body carrying yellow pigment to bleach and they lose their color very slowly, and in case they are bleached out, they indicate a very long period of egg production. According to the New Jersey station, the color leaves the outer ring of the scales, then leaves the entire scale, on the front of the shanks first, and, finally, after a longer and greater production leaves the scales on the rear of the shanks. A thoroughly bleached out shank on a yellow-colored bird of average size and average color, indicates that the fowl has been laying fairly heavy for a period of at least from 15 to 20 weeks.

When the hen or pullet ceases laying the yellow pigment immediately returns to the sections noted, its prevalence depending upon the length of her rest period.

Professor Lewis, of the New Jersey station, is authority for the statement that it requires approximately six eggs to free the vent entirely from the yellow pigment coloring matter, or from 10 to 12 days after the hen commences to lay from 10 to 15 eggs, or from 15 to 20 days, to entirely free the ear lobes from yellow coloring matter; from 30 to 40 eggs, or 60 to 75 days, to bleach the beak, or from 75 to 80 eggs, or 100 to 120 days, to entirely bleach out the shanks. The heavy layer, then, will carry bleached shanks through most of the laying year, and the 200-egg hens and the 300-egg hens (if such exist in farm flocks) will often be the poorest looking hens in the flock. The old standard of "nice, pretty yellow legs" falls by the wayside, and the only instance where it should be used in culling the farm flock is in the case of using it to secure the hens to send to market.

Physical tests, which are also best used in the careful, individual examination of the fowls, can be used to supplement the pigmentation test in selecting the layers. These physical tests are not only valuable in determining what hens are not laying or about to lay, but also in determining the future value of young pullets rapidly approaching maturity, but which have not as yet commenced to lay.

In taking up a fowl to examine, after having noted general characteristics as mentioned in a previous discussion, first examine the vent. You will note the condition of the skin, the general conformation of the abdominal region, the depth of keel or the distance from the point of the breast bone to the pubic or pelvic bones, two projecting bones readily located. This depth of keel is chiefly valuable because it denotes abdominal capacity— capacity to assimilate a sufficient quantity of food to make heavy laying possible. The fowl with a small capacity here is always a poor layer, simply because it is physically impossible for her to eat and assimilate sufficient food to keep up a fast gait of laying. The good layers always have a wide development here. Where the abdominal capacity is sufficient to admit four fingers of the hand between the point of the breast bone and the projection of the pubic bones a high producer is to be expected. It is safe to say that all hens that admit only two fingers in this region should be discarded as having a poor potential laying ability, whether they are now laying or not.

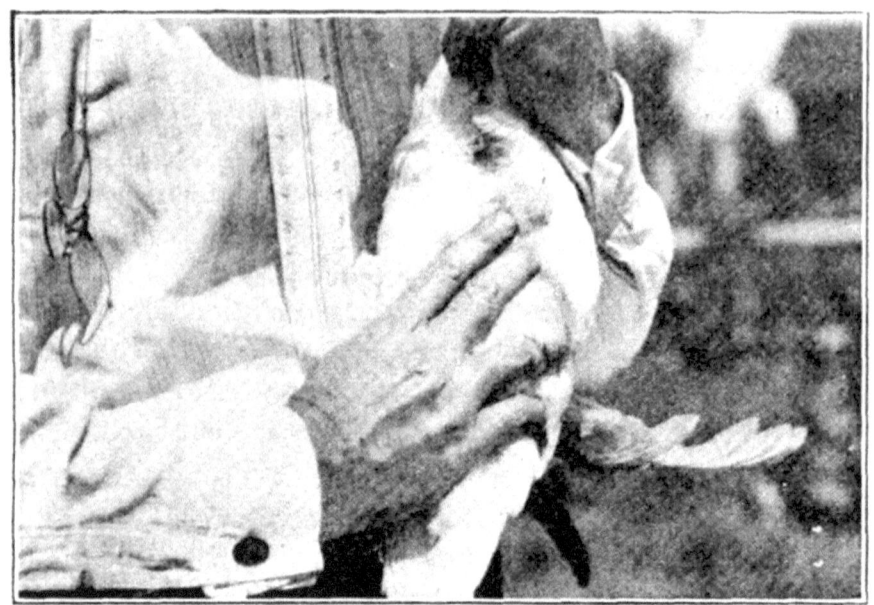

Fig. 62—A "Two-Finger" Layer, the Kind to Send to Market.

The span between the pubic bones can likewise be measured by the insertion of the fingers, as an indication of the laying habits of the hens. It must be remembered, however, that this test is chiefly of value for an indication of present performance.

Generally speaking, the spread between the pubic bones is the greatest in the high producers, varying somewhat in all hens. When the hen is not laying, as at molting period, the bones contract and a hen that is a good potential layer to keep for the coming year may show a spread of bone indicating, at the time, that she is a poor layer. Hence the need to take into consideration all the tests mentioned above, and to keep this in mind, if you are culling at a season of the year when most hens are molting. As a general rule, a "two finger" hen, one admitting the insertion of only two fingers between the pubic bones, is an inferior layer and should be discarded. Of course, any admitting less than two fingers should likewise be marketed. The good producers range above the "two finger" rule, some running to four fingers wide, but the great majority are "three finger" hens.

Careful examination of the hens as to type, condition, conformity to laying characteristics, and the tests mentioned above cannot fail to aid anyone in culling the non-producers from the flock with no chances of mistake, if the various tests are mastered and thoroughly in hand before the actual work commences. Culling under these tests will disclose many things about your flock that you never guessed before.

On the average, one-third of all farm hens are culls and are not producing sufficient eggs to pay for their own keep, let alone earn a profit. This fact was brought out in the Iowa culling demonstrations recently when 10 million cull hens were weeded out of farm flocks.

The following chart, issued by the U. S. Department of Agriculture, will serve to simplify the culling work. It classifies and places in a form easy to read at a glance the outstanding external characteristics of the good and bad layers:

Laying—Therefore Keep	Not Laying—Therefore Cull
HEALTH	**HEALTH.**
Good health. Good or fair condition of flesh. Active. Alert	Poor health, poor or thin condition of flesh, over-fat, broken down behind, listless, dumpy.
MOLT.	**MOLT.**
Not molting or just beginning to molt by the last of September or in October.	Molted or beginning to molt early in August.
COMB.	**COMB.**
Waxy, full of blood, red in color.	Shrunken, paler or duller red in color, comparatively hard, covered with whitish scales.
EYE.	**EYE.**
Prominent, bright, full of life.	Sunken, dull, listless in appear
PELVIC BONES.	**PELVIC BONES.**
Thin, flexible, spread apart more than the width of two fingers.	Thicker, less flexible, spread apart two fingers or less.
SIZE OF ABDOMEN.	**SIZE OF ABDOMEN.**
Spread of three or more fingers in the smaller breeds and four or	Spread of less than three fingers in the smaller breeds and less than

more in the larger breeds from pelvic bones to end of keel. Length of keel should also be considered. A hen with a long keel may have greater capacity than one with a short keel; but greater spread between pelvic bones and end of keel.

four in the larger breeds.

FLEXIBILITY OF ABDOMEN.

Soft, flexible.

FLEXIBILITY OF ABDOMEN.

Smaller, harder, less flexible.

APPEARANCE OF VENT.

Large, expanded, moist.

APPEARANCE OF VENT.

Comparatively small, hard, dry. puckered.

SHANK COLOR.

(Applies only to yellow-shanked breeds.) Pale yellow or white. Broody hens or those just recovered from broodiness may have yellow shanks, but should be kept if they have not begun to molt. A flock on good grass range will retain yellow shank color to a greater extent than those in bare yards.

SHANK COLOR.

(Applies only to yellow-shanked breeds.) Deep or medium yellow.

BEAK COLOR.

(Applies only to yellow-beaked breeds.) Pale or white.

BEAK COLOR.

(Applies only to yellow-skinned breeds.) Yellow or partly yellow.

VENT COLOR.

(Applies only to yellow-skinned breeds.) White or pink.

VENT COLOR.

(Applies only to yellow-skinned breeds.) Yellow.

Pelvic bones are the two bones side of the vent. which can be felt as points on each

CHAPTER XII

Care and Management for "Winter Eggs"

Details of First Importance— Regularity In Caring for the Flock — Keeping Things Clean— Should the Layers Have Range?

We have already given careful consideration to the problem of correctly housing the laying flock and to the correct manner in which to feed them for the best production. But a good house and a good ration are not the only considerations playing a part in the business of securing a high egg production. If they were, the laying hen would be, in truth, an "egg machine" and might be managed with a mathematical certainty as to the results and profits.

There are also other details entering into the care of the layers, particularly in the winter months, which are of prime importance in securing eggs. The most important of these is the water supply. It has long since been established that between 70 and 75 per cent of an egg is water. Many people give considerable attention to the matter of feeding the correct ration, who are indifferent about the water supply; in other words, they are paying the bulk of their attention towards supplying the ingredients from which the hen manufactures a small part of the egg. If she does not have the other elements, that egg will not be forthcoming no matter how good the housing, how good the ration or how good her breeding. This is what is meant when it is said that the problem now is to "feed out the lay already bred into the hens."

During the winter months the maintenance of a constant supply of fresh water is particularly trying, especially in severe weather when the tendency is for it to freeze within a few minutes after being placed in the pans. One can, at this season, soon satisfy himself as to the importance of water in the egg ration by carefully watering one pen or flock of layers, seeing that the water never freezes in that pen, and by watering only twice a day another pen containing the same number of layers. The first pen will greatly outlay the second and the only difference is in the amount of water supplied.

Since the labor element is great in maintaining the water supply in freezing weather, the farmer or poultryman should by all means install founts or watering devices which will not freeze. These come in various designs, some of them utilizing a vacuum principle similar to fireless cookers, and it is claimed that they will not freeze, but it should be noted that hot water has to be placed in them the night before and it is claimed that it will be kept from freezing for 24 hours. We have no quarrel with these founts and believe that they are a success, but we have had excellent results from another type.

This type of fount is simply a large galvanized receptacle for the water, made of galvanized iron, which contains a chamber in the bottom for an ordinary oil lamp which is refilled once each day. No large flame is necessary, as a small flame will prevent the water freezing even in very severe weather. We have found this fount to be extremely satisfactory and to solve the problem, as the fount itself is sufficiently large to require filling only once each day and it will serve a flock of 100 to 300 hens nicely. Smaller sizes can be purchased from any poultry supply dealer for smaller pens.

Another detail which often has an important influence on the egg production is the matter of oyster shell. The hens need a tremendous amount of lime in their ration if they are to continue to produce eggs day after day. Oyster shell is the most economical and desirable manner in which to supply this and you will find the hens eating enormous quantities of it. They seem to eat greedily of it at times as if it were grain, and we have always found that they prefer it to grit.

A failure of the supply of oyster shell in the shell boxes is always noticeable in a slump in the egg production for a few days following. Many times when our hens have undergone a decrease in the number of eggs laid on a given day that was hard to explain, and we searched around for the cause, we have found that the shell hopper had been inadvertently allowed to go "dry." If anyone desires to test the truth of this fact, all he has to do is to take the shell hopper away from hens that are on full laying schedule for a day or two and note the result. We do not mean to say that they will all promptly stop laying, but the effect of the absence of the shell will be noticeable for several days afterwards.

CHAPTER XII

And, of course, grit is another necessity that must not be overlooked. It is not as important as the shell, because the oyster shell may, for a time, take the place of it, and the fowls may even get along fairly well for a time without any grit at all, but it is a necessity nevertheless.

Good, clean, deep litter is a prime necessity for the laying hens. One might as well try to keep ducks out of water as to try and keep laying hens successfully in the winter without using a litter in the poultry house. There are a number of different substances recommended for litter in the laying house, but we have found none that seems to be as satisfactory as good, clean straw. And this is something which every farmer has right at hand.

The litter must be renewed frequently. This does not mean that new straw can be piled on top of the old dirty litter. It means that the old litter must be removed, the floors swept, and the new litter put in. If one is careful in his movements and works in one pen at a time, he can accomplish the work without unduly agitating the hens. Always be quiet and slow in your movements when around the hens. A frightened hen is not likely to prove a steady, consistent layer.

Tests have recently been conducted at certain stations looking to the value of good, clean litter and it was found that where dirty litter was allowed to accumulate in the laying houses that the egg production slumped, and that as soon as clean, sweet litter was placed in the same houses, the production immediately increased in amount.

Regularity In Caring for the Flock

What we have said about regularity in caring for the young stock applies with equal force to caring for the laying hens. One cannot be indifferent and slip-shod in his work here and expect any great records from the layers. Regularity in feeding and care is of the first importance to the farmer or poultryman because it is through this practice that the best results are obtained and, consequently, the best profits.

There should be a regular time for each duty in regard to the laying flock and then the work will be more likely to be done promptly. The droppings should be gathered from the droppings board each morning before six 'clock, as this is the best time of the whole day. The hens are then all busy in the litter getting their breakfast and are less likely to be disturbed, as few, if any, of them are then on the nests.

Later the main morning feeding can be done, if it has not already been taken care of, the water founts filled and the lamps serving them, if you have anti-freeze founts, trimmed and filled. If the mash hoppers are low and need to be filled this work can be done. The flock will then require no more attention until noon when the sprouted oats or other green food is fed and the first gathering of eggs made. In freezing weather, the eggs will have to be gathered oftener to prevent freezing in the nests.

During the afternoon, no further attention will be required until about 3:30 or 4 o'clock when the evening grain ration is given. This should be fed early enough so that the hens can go to roost with full crops. If artificial lighting is followed this feeding can be delayed until two hours before the lights are turned off for the night. The eggs are then gathered, the nests closed up so that the birds cannot roost in them, and the work for the day is over.

Regularity and attention to every detail, however trivial, is the great cornerstone of success in poultry keeping. This is even more important where the poultry work is a sideline to some other occupation.

Keeping Things Clean

The importance of keeping things clean in the laying house is much greater than many people imagine. We sometimes think that it is the truest index of whether or not the individual will succeed, or is a success, is to know whether they make a practice of cleaning up the droppings in the laying house at least every other day and regularly scald the feed and water dishes and give the roosts a thorough spraying.

It is a singular fact that on those farms where the droppings are allowed to accumulate under the roosts and go for weeks before they are taken away, that there you will find the attendant having trouble in some way with his flock. It may not be the droppings that are to blame, but there is an indication here by which we can judge the character of the man. And it indicates a tendency to slip-shod methods.

On the other hand, the farms you visit where cleanliness is the first rule, there you will generally find the most successful poultry people and nice flocks of contented layers busy shelling out the eggs.

A few minutes every morning will suffice to keep the laying houses clean and will, in the end, save much time and labor. It is also one of the surest preventives of disease and, from that standpoint alone, is worth while.

Should the Layers Have Range?

Where the laying flock is housed in any one of the laying houses illustrated in the Chapter on Buildings, or others embodying the same principles, range should be denied the layers during the winter and spring months; at least until the ground is dry and the weather settled.

Hens that are allowed to run in and out of the laying houses become dissatisfied on days when they have to be kept penned up on account of the weather and they do not produce the results they do where they are confined to the houses all the time.

We have demonstrated to our own satisfaction that a hen with wet feet will not lay as well as the one kept in a dry, well-ventilated laying house. It is common practice for farmers to turn the hens out whenever possible and it will be hard for those in the habit to keep the hens penned up in the laying house. But the better results in egg yield will justify it.

Another reason why the layers should be denied free range during the main laying season is that they produce a larger percentage of soiled eggs at this time. They get their feet and feathers wet or muddy and then when they get on the nest they not only soil their own eggs but those already in the nests. Hens with wet feathers or muddy feet cannot produce clean eggs. And these eggs cannot be washed and sent to market as "firsts." The candler will spot them in a minute and they will be classed as "dirties" and will bring a price much lower than top on the market.

This is another reason for keeping the laying house clean and the droppings gathered up as often as possible. It makes the production of pure clean eggs possible and does not penalize you by a large number of "dirties."

Where the laying flock has the proper amount of room and has a good straw litter to work in, and is given a good ration supplemented with green food at noon, there is absolutely no advantage whatever to be gained from allowing them free range. Instead, the egg yield is certain to be less because more of the ration consumed will be going to supply the bodily needs of the hens caused by them running all over the place. In other words, they will be "running off" the energy that might otherwise be going to eggs. The best plan is to keep the layers confined to the laying house throughout the laying season.

CHAPTER XIII

Artificial Lighting for Winter Eggs

Purpose— Results— Costs— Systems One May Use— How to Run Lights— Dangers and Pitfalls to Avoid — Automatic Regulation

Artificial lighting will be a new wrinkle to a great many people. And a good many others who have heard about it haven't gotten over the idea that it is a great joke or hoax. But the joke, if there is any, is on the fellow who will not take seriously to the idea that artificial lighting will increase winter egg production.

By artificial lighting we mean that we use lights in the laying house during the short days of fall, winter and early spring for the purpose of increasing the normal working day of the hens. It has been found that the average short winter day does not give the average pullet or hen sufficient time in which to eat and assimilate sufficient feed to make heavy egg production possible. It is well known that if a hen goes to roost at night with an unlaid egg in her system that the tendency is to reabsorb it and it goes to fat. By simply increasing the length of the working day through artificial lighting of hen houses, we make it possible for the hens not so efficient in the digestion and assimilation of their feed to complete the process and deposit their eggs in the nests before going to roost.

Does this sound foolish to you? Then stop to consider that the best laying season of the whole year is in the spring and early summer months. Why is this?

It must be due to the natural conditions obtaining at that time. We have, for years, sought to imitate these natural conditions, especially in making up the elements going into the ration, in the thought that if we could so feed them in the winter months that we would be likely to get an increased egg production. And this has been true, but soon the investigators determined to make the hen's working day in the winter just like the day in spring and the moment they tried that they were accorded a revelation.

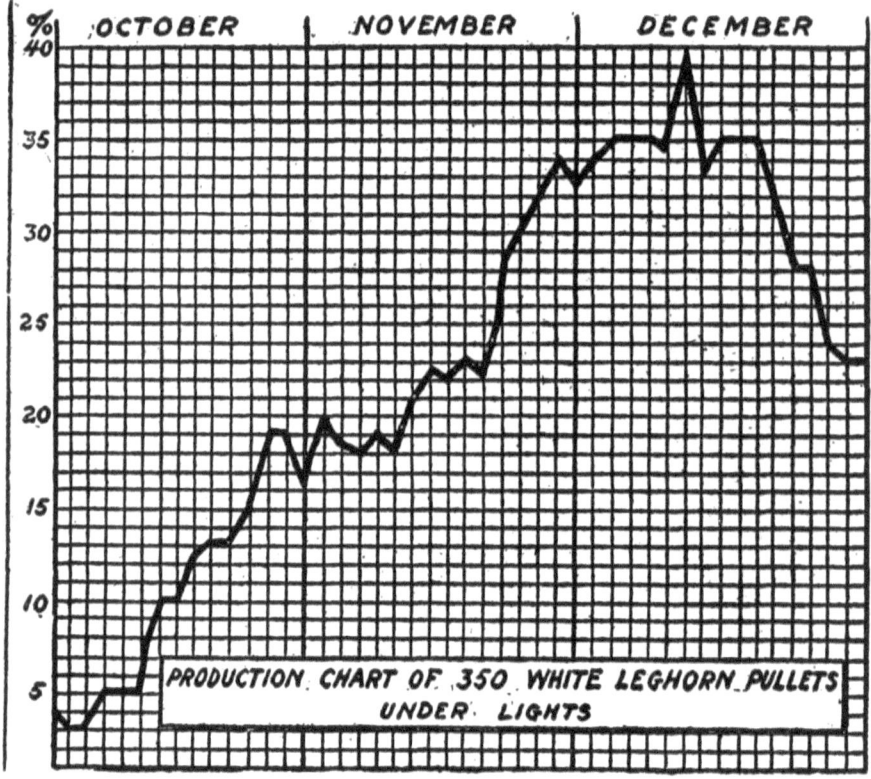

Fig. 63—Line Shows Increase in Egg Production After Artificial Lighting Was Started.

Do not fall into the error of thinking, as so many people thoughtlessly do, that by artificial lighting we "fool" the hens into thinking it is daylight and they then go and lay their eggs. Such an expression only reveals the stupendous ignorance of these people for the processes by which the egg is produced. There is no "fooling" about it; it is a simple matter of supplying a given amount of raw material and affording sufficient time to make it possible for the efficient hen to complete the process and deliver the goods.

The purpose of artificial lighting is to lengthen the day in winter to correspond to the normal working day of the hens in spring, in order to make it possible for them to eat and assimilate their feed to better advantage, resulting in an increased egg production.

Results

Of course, people are interested in results. That is the one safe method by which the value of an innovation can be judged. What are the results of artificial laying? Do they justify the installation of lights in the laying house?

We have talked to dozens of farmers and poultry raisers all over the Middle West who are using artificial lighting in their laying houses and without exception they have all stated that it greatly increased winter egg production. The various results obtained ranged from 30 per cent to 45 per cent increase in the egg production in the winter months.

Hugo Anderson, the Minnesota poultryman mentioned in an earlier chapter, said: "Isn't artificial lighting a great help? I wouldn't be without the lights for anything! I commence to run the lights on the first of November and run them through the winter 14 hours a day, right straight through until they are no longer necessary. I commence the lights at 6 a. m. and run them until 8 p. m. Of course during the day when they are not needed, they are turned off." The lights have been responsible for Mr. Anderson securing a 40 per cent egg production from a flock of 1,000 old hens in November.

Mrs. Etta Bechtel, an Iowa farm woman who uses artificial lighting, states that her egg production increased 30 per cent immediately after the lights were installed.

In a test conducted by a New York State commercial poultryman to determine the value and comparative returns of artificial lighting as compared with the old method, 70 pullets were placed in a pen under artificial lights. Another flock of 350 pullets were not given the lights. The 70 pullets laid 1,108 eggs during the test and the 350 pullets laid 1,917 eggs. The market value of the eggs laid by the 79 pullets under lights was $47.01 and of the eggs laid by the 350 pullets not under lights $83.94. The value of the product produced per bird was 23 2-3 cents each for the

350 pullets not under lights and 69 cents each for the 70 pullets under lights.

In tests conducted at Cornell University extending through a whole year where an equal number of hens of the same age were placed in identical houses, lights being given to one pen and not to the other, it was found that the average annual production of the lighted pen was 38.3 per cent and of the unlighted pen the production was 30.2 per cent for the year. In the case of a similar group of pullets, the lighted pen showed an annual production of 41.95 per cent and the unlighted pen 34.28 per cent. The clear gain in favor of lights based on the average of the two pens of 7.9 per cent. The cash return would have been even greater because the lights brought the great bulk of the production at the season of the year when market prices were the highest

Costs

What does it cost to run artificial lights, That is a question that will instantly present itself to the average person. The cost has varied under different conditions, but in almost every instance, it is surprisingly low. The cost will depend upon the system used, the number of lights run and the efficiency of the burner or bulb.

D. E. Carlson, who keeps a flock of 1,000 Leghorn layers as a sideline to running a 115-acre Iowa farm, stated to the author that his electric lights cost him from $2 to $3 per month. He uses a 75-watt bulb in each pen 20 feet square in his Iowa Semi-Monitor House.

Mrs. Etta Bechtel uses gas lights which are piped into each pen and her son stated to the writer that the entire cost of the plant, including the lights in the residence and elsewhere amounted to $1.25 per week. These lights supply 1,000 winter layers, and as soon as they were installed the production increased 30 per cent!

In a test conducted at the New York State School of Agriculture at Cobleskill, 35 Leghorn pullets and 30 Leghorn hens were supplied electric lights during the three winter months of November, December, 1918, and January, 1919, at a cost of $2.93. In the meantime, they returned a profit above feed and cost of light per bird of $1.59 for the three months.

CHAPTER XIII

Systems One Mat Use

Any number of lighting systems are available to the farmer who desires to give the hens the benefit of artificial lighting. Electricity, gas, or oil lanterns are all good and will serve to secure the results in mind. Some of these systems are naturally better than others, when viewed from all angles.

Electric lights are probably the most economical in cost for maintenance, and they are certainly the most economical from the standpoint of labor involved in managing them. They can be automatically regulated by means of alarm clock devices so that the lights will be turned on and off at the proper time, making it unnecessary for the attendant to get up to turn on the lights or make the round of the pens to light the lights where lanterns or gas lights are used. Then the fire danger is reduced to a minimum.

Gas lights and gas lanterns may be used, however, and will accomplish the same purpose. The small high candle power gasoline lanterns are also good, but they have the unhappy faculty of getting clogged up because of the dust in the air and cause trouble.

Where one has a connection to an electric current, or can install a farm lighting plant generating electricity, it is,, by all odds, the most desirable method to use in supplying the lights.

How TO Run Lights

Tests have been made of lights under almost every kind of a condition to determine the best way in which to run them. The lights have been started in the morning and run until early in the evening; they have not been started at all in the morning and have been run until late at night, and again they have been started about 6 a. m. and run until 9 p. m.— all with the idea of determining what plan would produce the best results.

It would seem from these tests, which were conducted at Cornell University, and which covered an entire year in extent, that the best time in which to run the lights is from 6 a. m. until 9 p. m., shutting off the lights during the day when not needed. This gives one a working day of 15 hours, which is normal, as based on the normal period of daylight in the season of the year when egg production is usually at its highest peak.

We have heard of no method of running the lights that gives better results.

The lights should be started not later than November first and run right straight through without a break until the normal period of daylight merges into these hours and makes their use unnecessary. This is for the purpose of preventing the hens or pullets being prematurely thrown into a molt through the sudden shutting off of the lights.

Dangers and Pitfalls to Avoid

The greatest danger of artificial lighting is the ever present menace of throwing the pullets or hens into a premature molt. If regularity in the care of hens ever meant anything it certainly means everything here. The attendant must make up his or her mind that the lights are to be run on a regular schedule that does not vary two minutes day after day, or they had best let the lights alone. These irregularities have a tendency to throw the hens into premature molts which interfere with the egg records.

Another tendency is to push the hens a little too hard, and it is apt to result in leg weakness and even entire loss of use of the legs. This comes from undue forcing through running the lights too long and if there is any indication of it, the lights should either be cut down one hour in the length they are run, gradually of course, or the feed fed in light litter for several days. Sometimes, forcing the hens to work too hard in the litter causes this trouble, which is undoubtedly a form of paralysis.

CHAPTER XIII

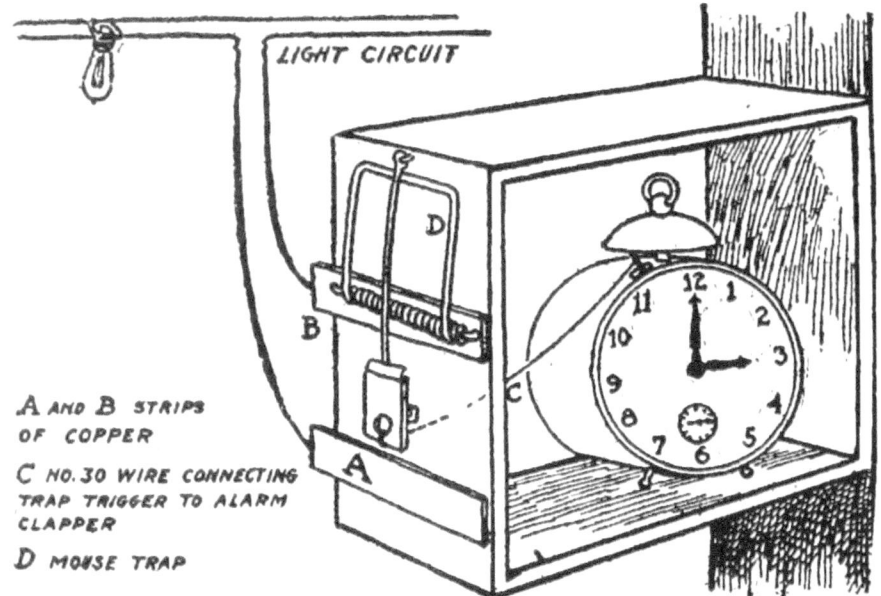

A AND B STRIPS OF COPPER
C NO. 30 WIRE CONNECTING TRAP TRIGGER TO ALARM CLAPPER
D MOUSE TRAP

Fig. 64—Simple Alarm Clock Arrangement to Automatically Turn on Lights, Perfected by Irving King,, an Iowa Poultryman.

Moderation is always the best policy. One cannot fly very far in the face of Nature without inviting disaster. Common sense must be the rule in running the lights and the first sensible thought is that the efficiency of the laying flock must not be broken down by unwise and injudicious use of the lighting system.

Automatic Regulation of Lights

The accompanying sketch shows a simple plan whereby the lights may be automatically turned on through the use of an alarm clock and a mouse trap. This device was first made by Irving King, an Iowa poultry raiser. It is simplicity in itself and the sketch explains the principle on which it works. One point should be kept in mind and that is that the string attached to the clapper of the clock and the trigger of the trap must not be taut, but, at the same time, taut enough to jiggle the trigger and spring it.

CHAPTER XIV

Marketing Farm Eggs Successfully

Shipping Eggs— How to Pack for Shipment— Use of Cartons— Grading Eggs— Private Trade— Advertising

The most satisfactory way in which to market eggs produced on a large scale is to market them in a wholesale way; that is, they are shipped to commission dealers or jobbers who, in turn, parcel them out to the retailers or consumers. The fundamental work of the egg farmer is that of a producer and unless it is possible for him to join a co-operative egg marketing association made possible by the presence of a large number of shippers in his locality, it will be best for him to utilize the existing marketing agencies. He cannot go into the merchandising side of the business to very great an extent without running a risk of sacrificing something on the production side.

As a general rule, the sale of eggs produced on a large scale cannot be successfully transacted on the local market. The consumption of the average local market is limited and unless one lives near a good-sized city the risk is that at times there will be no demand for the eggs produced. To insure an outlet, then, it is wise to cater to the market of the larger cities where the demand is always constant and to ship the eggs in wholesale lots rather than to attempt to parcel them out a dozen at a time around home.

This will insure, in the long run, a better return for the eggs than the local markets will afford, even though the eggs may be marketed at retail around home, because the level of prices at wholesale is generally higher than at retail out in the country districts where they are produced and where eggs are comparatively plentiful.

The New York City market stands first as the best market for white eggs; by this we mean that the principal demand is for white eggs and that it is the white eggs which are most likely to command a premium in price. Boston demands a brown egg and prefers it to the white egg. Buffalo and Detroit prefer white eggs. Always ascertain the preference of the market in regard to white or brown eggs and then cater to the markets which prefer the kind of eggs you are producing. There is no object in shipping your eggs to a market that does not care for them and that even goes to the extent of penalizing you for shipping them by paying you a lower price for them.

The reason for this preference for white or brown shelled eggs is often hard to understand or explain. It is probably due to habit more than anything else and when all the people in a given locality get in the habit of buying a white shelled egg it is hard to sell them anything else, or vice versa.

Eggs for market are shipped in egg cases holding 30 dozen eggs. The man with a flock of 1,000 layers on the side will have several cases in transit all the time. He will soon come to think no more of shipping his eggs to New York City than he would think of going to the neighboring town to do his trading. Market eggs generally go forward by express, in fact, it would be foolish to try and ship them any other way. Express rates are not high, it costing less than $1.50 per case to ship eggs from Iowa to New York City at the present time.

Select a good, reliable commission firm in the city to which you are shipping and as soon as you have found him to be reliable, stick to him. People who constantly change firms are in no way to get the best price for their product and are likely to fall into the hands of a dishonest concern before they get through.

CHAPTER XIV

Fig. 65—Egg Cartons Containing Your Farm Name Build Up a Demand for Your Eggs.

One can generally secure the names of reliable commission firms through advertisements in the poultry journals, by writing to other successful market egg producers in your state of whom you may learn, or by writing to the express agent in the city to which you wish to ship telling him that you desire to ship eggs and asking him to recommend a reliable dealer to you. Or you may ask your local banker or merchant to look in his Dun or Bradstreet directory for the names of reliable firms on the market and then write to each of them for particulars as to their service, how to pack for shipment, etc. If you will address a postal card to your express agent, he can secure for you from his company several pamphlets explanatory of the best manner in which to pack and mark eggs for shipment. These will be cheerfully furnished by the express company free of charge.

How TO Pack for Shipment

From a pamphlet issued by the American Railway, Express Company under the title, "The Right Way to Ship Eggs," we quote the following directions:

The losses due to broken eggs run into thousands of dollars each month.

It's partly our fault, and partly the shipper's.

Eggs shipped by express must necessarily be handled many times. They should be packed to stand ordinary handling. Our duty is to prevent rough handling.

We are asking shippers to prevent losses due to poor Packing and poor Marking.

Here are a few important rules of particular importance to shippers of eggs:—

Shipper's Safety Rules

Don't expose eggs to excessive cold or to heat. Store them in a cool, well-ventilated room.

Don't hold eggs too long before shipping. This causes excessive shrinkage.

Don't wash eggs for shipment. It removes Nature's protection, causing rapid decay.

Use good, secure Egg Cases.

Don't use Second-Hand Cases unless well reinforced. Flat strap iron is best, as it does not interfere with proper stowing of cases in cars, etc.

Don't use second-hand fillers.

Don't ship extra-large eggs with regular sizes. The standard filler is only 2 ¼ inches high. Eggs longer than 2 inches are almost certain to be broken.

Don't mix duck eggs and hen eggs in same ease. Keep for local use the irregular or imperfect eggs.

Don't fail to place a good level cushion of excelsior or some other such material, on the top and bottom of such ease.

Don't fail to nail the lids down firmly— an extra nail or two may save the loss of a dozen eggs.

About Marking

Remove or cancel all old marks on cases. Put shipper's name and address and consignee's name and address on each end of each case you ship. This will insure quick returns.

Mark with stencil, good substantial tags, or heavy address card, firmly tacked down.

If labels are used, paste them down securely. Mark the cases to denote the number of dozen therein.

Safety Rules for Express Employees

Insist on strict enforcement of the packing rules. See that crates are properly marked, all old marks removed. Handle eggs carefully. Guard against accidents. Keep lot shipments together. Keep cases of eggs right side up always. Keep eggs dry and away from heat or extreme cold. Deliver promptly.

Express Classification Rules

"Standard egg cases or carriers (sometimes termed 'gift' cases) must be made of hard wood of not less than the following dimensions:

"Sides, top, and bottom, three-sixteenths of an inch in thickness; ends and center partitions, seven-sixteenths of an inch in thickness; and end cleats, one and one-half by seven-sixteenths of an inch in thickness.

"Second-hand 'standard' or 'gift' cases or carriers (cases or carriers which have already been used in transportation of eggs, and re-used) must be strapped with iron, wire or wooden straps on the sides and bottom at each end.

"Eggs packed in orange, lemon, shoe or other miscellaneous boxes or in 'standard' cases or carriers which are too frail to stand transportation will not he accepted.

"All trays and dividing boards must be of hard calendar strawboard, weighing not less than three pounds to the set, and of sufficient size to fill the compartments to prevent shifting; the bottom dividing boards must be placed next to the eggs and on top of a cushion of excelsior, cork shavings, cut straw or corrugated strawboard cushion; the top dividing boards to be placed next to the eggs, and covered with sufficient excelsior, cork shavings, cut straw or corrugated cushion to hold the contents firmly in place.

"Eggs in pulphoard cushion carton filers packed in standard egg cases will be accepted for shipment at same rates and estimated weight as when packed with ordinary fillers.

"Cases or carriers, whether new or second-hand, containing second-hand fillers, will not be accepted, except that pulpboard moulded fillers may be used as often as same are in proper condition."

Use of Cartons

The inherent value of goods— the utility value— plays but a small part in determining the sale price, in a great many commodities. This is particularly true in the case of food products. If it were not true, for instance, we would be content to buy coats with several sizes of buttons sewed on them or made from different pieces of cloth. If it were not true, we should find styles playing little favor in the clothing business. If it were not true, we would buy our rolled oats in bulk or our cookies in bulk, rather than in nice, attractive cartons.

There is another consideration, perhaps several considerations, which play a large part in determining the sale price of a food commodity, as distinguished from other commodities of like kind. One of these is attractiveness. We buy largely through our sense of sight; if food commodities are clean, attractive and uniform in size or quality, they look "good" and we buy them. On the other hand, similar products just as fresh and valuable from the standpoint of nourishment, but less attractive do not appeal to us.

Suppose we apply this thought to market eggs. If you have to buy market eggs and walk into a market or store and have a choice of three grades of eggs, (1) dirty, irregular mixed brown and white eggs, (2) graded eggs all white or all brown, (3) graded white or brown eggs placed in cartons stamped with a guaranty of quality and the producer's name and address, which lot of eggs will appeal to you the most? It is certain that if you have any element of choice at all you will buy your eggs from the last two classes. The more discriminating city buyers are in the habit of buying standardized, branded goods and they soon learn that it

Fig. 66—Carefully Selected Eggs Ready for Shipment to New York Market.

CHAPTER XIV

does not pay, in the long run, to buy any other kind. So the vast majority of them are willing to pay a premium for a product that they can depend upon. If you wish to understand the motives back of the city buyer, and to cash in on it, you have the whole story here in a nutshell. These are fundamental economic factors that apply in the determination of commodity sale prices and those who succeed in securing the highest prices for their products are the ones who recognize these factors and cater to them.

Many Middle Western poultry raisers are shipping market eggs to the New York City markets and oftentimes receive a premium over existing market prices ranging from 5 cents to 15 cents per dozen. The reason is found in the fact that they grade their eggs to size and weight, primarily, and sometimes they pack their eggs in their own cartons. There is no other "secret" to the matter.

An egg may be an egg and it may take only 12 to make a dozen, but for all that there is a difference. That difference may not appear to be worth the "bother" to many busy people, but it is just such little differences as this that define the maximum success. The egg farmer has but to take a leaf from the experience of the business man in order to profit. The package idea is well established in all lines of business. From time immemorial we have had rolled oats, gingersnaps, prunes, raisins, dried fruits, oyster crackers and candy in bulk. Practically all the progress that has been made in our merchandising in half a century has been in the discarding of bulk commodities and the adoption of package commodities, followed by the advertising of these brands.

The package idea has been applied to the marketing of eggs for some years, but it is only recently that individual egg farmers have awakened to the great opportunity and commenced to do it themselves. For years, it has been done by the packers and the egg dealers, merely because it increased the profit to be gained from the eggs they handled to place them in cartons containing some such caption as "Extra Fancy," "Strictly Fresh," or "Selected Eggs."

Grading Eggs

One dirty egg in a dozen, or one embryo chick, will absolutely "spoil" that dozen eggs in the mind of the average buyer and cause the said buyer to return them to the storekeeper. The United States Department of

Agriculture has said that the preventable loss suffered by egg farmers throughout the country is 17 per cent of all eggs sent to market. This runs into millions of dollars in each state each year. Seven and one-half per cent of this loss comes through a failure to produce infertile eggs for market, resulting in partially developed chicks being formed through the eggs becoming heated, or from rotten eggs. An infertile egg is an egg having no male germ and they can be produced and practically all of this loss eliminated by simply removing cock birds from the laying houses.

Two per cent of this loss comes from dirty eggs. Clean eggs can be produced by keeping the nests clean, keeping the dropping boards and litter clean and confining the laying hens to good houses so that they do not have range in wet weather. A hen with wet feet or one laying in a dirty nest will result in dirty eggs. You cannot "slip one over" by washing the eggs, either. That does not fool the candler or the trade and it results in the more rapid deterioration of the egg.

The five grades of eggs most commonly made by egg dealers are as follows:

1. Extra Selects.— Eggs in this class must be strictly fresh, large in size, clean shelled, free from stains and unwashed, contents full and whites strong. This grade always brings a premium, ranging all the way from 2 1/2 cents per dozen upward.

2. Firsts.— Eggs in this grade must be reasonably fresh, large in size, clean shelled, but not as full and fresh as the extra selects.

3. Trade.— Eggs of this grade are put up to meet the trade demands and are usually for immediate consumption. They may be nearly equal to firsts in quality, but are smaller in size and oftentimes are slightly soiled. dirty and stained, but for immediate use they are as good as firsts. They generally sell for less than firsts, and about the price of current receipts.

4. Seconds.— This grade includes eggs that will not come in any of the better grades. They are composed generally of stale, shrunken eggs, eggs small in size, slightly heated and slightly soiled. They must be edible, free from rots, spots or bad eggs. The price of seconds is usually 2 cents or more below that of trade eggs.

5. Dirties.— This grade includes eggs that are too dirty, soiled and stained to come in any of the above grades. Washed eggs are usually

placed with dirties, because they deteriorate about as rapidly as dirty eggs. Generally the price for dirties is about the same as that of seconds, varying with the demand.

Eggs graded for the best grade you have should weigh not less than 24 ounces to the dozen; if they can be graded higher, it will pay to do so. Oftentimes, where yearling Leghorns or Minorcas are carried, it is possible to grade the best eggs to 26 to 30 ounces to the dozen and it pays to grade them as high as possible. Pullet eggs should be graded to 24 ounces and sold as such.

Private Trade

Where the egg farmer lives near a large city it is often desirable to develop an outlet for the eggs through private channels. The average farmer, however, generally objects to running a delivery system or to peddling his product from house to house. This must, of course, be settled by the individual but many have found a profit in it and have even charged five to ten cents above market prices for their eggs and then been unable to supply the demand.

This sort of work calls for more than usual sales and advertising ability, but it is not beyond the realm of possibility. It is not hard to popularize your brand of eggs, if you pack them in your own cartons, and then advertise them properly, dwelling upon the purity of your product, as compared with that of the average farm egg produced by hens having the run of manure heaps and feed lots.

Hugo Anderson, the Minnesota poultryman we have mentioned,

Fig 67—Grade the Eggs Carefully for the Best Price.

packs his eggs in cartons, carefully grading them to size and weight and disposes of his entire product to a Duluth department store. His pullet eggs are packed in special cartons and sold at five cents per dozen less than his best grade. He has more of a demand than he can supply. Some such arrangement might be worked out in almost any city, but one must have a sufficient volume to be able to furnish some eggs all the time, as these stores do not care to cater to a certain trade and then be unable to supply the demand at least partially. Mr. Anderson maintains a flock of 3,500 layers on his plant, so one can get some idea of the demand he has developed.

Advertising

No advertising of market eggs is necessary unless you are catering to the private trade and are anxious to build up more of a demand for your product among retail customers. The best and most economical way in which this can be done is through direct-by-mail methods, such as letters, circulars and descriptive folders addressed direct to the prospects.

Fresh eggs are something that every city householder is looking for and if you address such matter direct to them telling how they can get in touch with you to secure your packaged and guaranteed product, you

CHAPTER XIV

will have very little advertising to do in order to secure sufficient demand. This is especially true if you are willing to establish a delivery system and bring the eggs in regularly, at least once each week.

CHAPTER XV

How to Sell and Advertise Stock

Surplus Stock— How to Pack and Ship Hatching Eggs— Where and How to Advertise

Those who are producing market eggs and are building up a flock of high producers through intelligent breeding are soon going to have the flock at such a point that it will not be profitable to sell the surplus cockerels on the general market for broilers. The higher the records made by the layers, especially where pedigree breeding is done and trapnesting carefully followed, the more valuable the surplus birds are going to be for sale as breeders.

The yearling hens which have served for layers or breeders can be more profitably marketed for breeding birds than they can be realized on as market fowl. It is not out of the ordinary at all to dispose of all yearling hens in this way for not less than two dollars each, ranging on up according to the reputation of the flock and the breeder.

During the normal hatching season in the spring months, it will be possible for the farmer to market his eggs in the form of hatching eggs or baby chicks at several times the price they normally bring at this season for market purposes. This tends to secure, the year around, the maximum price for the product and, therefore, to insure the highest profit from the operations.

But in order to do this it is necessary that the public be acquainted with what you are doing. You are going to have to create a demand for your stock and hatching eggs through careful advertising and through careful breeding in building up a strain that will do well in the hands of customers. After all, the best advertisement is the satisfied customer.

One cannot build a business of this sort over night. It comes slowly but the great advantage of advertising is in its cumulative effect— it constantly piles up a reputation for you which, if backed up by the right kind of goods, will continue to work for you day and night as long as you are in business. And, as a general rule, a man will be forced into the breeding business more and more as time goes on, even though he might have started out originally with the idea that he would confine his attention exclusively to the production of eggs for market. But profit attracts, almost compels one, to move in this direction in order to secure proper outlet for his surplus stock.

A Minnesota farmer who has since become one of the largest utility Leghorn breeders in the country told the author of his early experiences along this line. "I started out with the intention of producing eggs for market," he said. "I felt that I did not care to go into the breeding business or to sell hatching eggs or stock because I didn't want to advertise and carry on a correspondence with prospective customers.

"But I was forced to bigger things and have constantly been forced to bigger things. Today, I am carrying on a general business in which I supply a trademarked egg to the general market in the neighboring city; I sell thousands of my surplus young cockerels every year for breeding purposes, and I market an average of 50,000 baby chicks each season, shipping them all over the Union. I also raise 12-week 's-old pullets for sale in midsummer. Last year I sold 1,000 of these at one swipe to another poultryman for $2.50 each cash ! "You see, you can't keep from going in this direction when it is the one way that offers a profit for the surplus stock. No man can make a profit selling stock on the general market and it hasn't been profitable for two decades."

How TO Pack and Ship Hatching Eggs

One of the problems confronting the beginner in purebred poultry work is the matter of properly packing hatching eggs for shipment. There are any number of containers advertised on the market, and any number of plans proposed by those having more or less experience in this work. The beginner, as a rule, follows the course of least resistance and often finds that he has ac-

Fig. 68—Roadside Signs Will Attract Attention to Your Farm.

CHAPTER XV

cepted poor advice, which has caused him to sustain severe losses, the chief one of which is the loss of prestige among his customers.

Eggs that are shipped to various parts of the country for hatching purposes must be packed and handled in the most careful manner in order to insure the maximum results. Rough handling or breakage often seriously affects the hatching qualities of the eggs. Hatching eggs may be shipped at the present time either by express or by parcel post, but in either instance the amount of rough handling which is bound to occur in transit is so great that the shipper must use every possible precaution in packing to be sure that the eggs are properly insulated in order to reduce to a minimum the effect of such treatment.

We have found in discussion with a number of practical poultry men and women of the Middle West that the commonly accepted method of packing hatching eggs, one which is sure to give the best results, is to use large baskets similar to ordinary bushel baskets for containers. These baskets come in various sizes and may be purchased from certain manufacturers for the purpose of shipping hatching eggs. The sizes ordinarily run from two settings or 30 eggs up to several hundred.

One practical poultry woman, who ships eggs every season, informs us that she has found the basket container to be the best from her standpoint. She wraps the eggs in a piece of paper, and then uses excelsior around these eggs so that a perfect ball is formed. A layer of excelsior is placed on the bottom of the basket are packed in the center, a wall of excelsior being around the side of the basket and over the top. The best cover for this basket is a strip of burlap sewed into the basket frame or some other kind of heavy cloth. Some breeders, however, have used ordinary slated covers nailed fast to the basket with good results.

Fig. 69—One Way of Advertising Your Products

This experience has been borne out by a number of other breeders and seems to be worthy of passing on to our readers. Another very good way to pack eggs is to use heavy cardboard containers or small boxes, sufficiently large in which to pack the eggs shipped and still afford room for proper insulation. One of the best packed containers of hatching eggs we ever received came from an eastern breeder in one of these cardboard boxes or containers. The eggs were packed in fine sawdust and chaff. A layer of this material was placed in the bottom on top of several thicknesses of newspapers. Then came the eggs, which were all carefully surrounded by sufficient sawdust and chaff to prevent them touching each other. A layer was placed across the top and then several thicknesses of newspaper to make the entire package snug and unsusceptible to shocks or jolts.

Another shipment of eggs coming from a Michigan breeder, came in an ordinary market basket, which was insulated with long grass. The grass was used in the same manner that the farm woman mentioned uses excelsior or the eastern breeder mentioned used sawdust and chaff.

The exact type of packing material is not essential, so much as is the manner in which the package is packed. Any of these materials will afford excellent results, provided the shipper is very careful to see that the eggs are packed in a careful manner and so that it is impossible for them to "give" or jostle against each other.

The greatest caution should be used in securing containers large enough to properly handle the eggs. Most people come to grief because they use containers too small to afford proper insulation. The container used should be at least 50 per cent larger than the size generally advertised to hold the eggs.

Where and How to Advertise

Where and how shall I advertise my surplus stock and eggs? is a question commonly asked by the beginner. This is a question that can seldom be answered satisfactorily for the reason that one kind of advertising may produce a good business for one man and be an utter failure for another. And, again, one medium or paper in which the advertisement is run, may produce all the business one breeder can handle and not bring a single dollar to another breeder. There are many considerations entering into the business of advertising which can influence the results. But there is one rule which should ever be followed and that is that persistency is the best way to succeed at advertising. There is no profit in running one ad and then sitting down to wait for the business. Competition is too keen in this day and age for success to come that easily. John Wanamaker, the great merchant prince, who ought to know something about advertising, once said that it is the last business in the world in which the quitter should indulge.

Where shall I advertise? That is, indeed, a pertinent question, with all this mass of advertising media offered. The very first thought to keep in mind, in selecting a paper in which to advertise, is the average type of reader taking that paper. Are these readers likely to be prospects for what you have to sell? If not, that paper is going to be a costly medium in which to run your advertisement for it will not secure the sort of reader distribution that can reasonably be counted upon to bring you a fair amount of business. Having decided upon a paper which appeals to the class of buyers you think most likely to be interested in your product, the next point to consider is the circulation or the number of readers which the paper has in its field. If it does not have a fair standing or prestige in its field, then it is likely to prove an unprofitable advertising medium because the low circulation indicates that there is a low reader-interest in the paper. If not, there would be more people reading and discussing that paper.

You want to secure, then, circulation in the field to which you wish to appeal and to secure as much of it as possible. If any one paper stands out preeminent in reader-interest that is a good paper in which to advertise, because people are not merely "taking" it, they are reading it.

State farm papers should be the first step in the advertising chain forged by the farmer-poultryman, and a careful inquiry among those who have succeeded in this direction reveals, almost without exception, that that is just the way they worked it out in their own practical experience. And, remember to pick the papers with the best circulations whenever possible.

Poultry journals and breed journals are also good mediums, but one often has to spend some good money before he discovers the individual journals which are the best "pullers" of business. There is one pretty good indication which can be kept in mind at all times and that is the volume of advertising which these papers carry. The papers which carry the best volume of advertising indicate on their face the ones which are "pulling" the best for the other breeders. But, when you insert your copy in those papers you are going to have to make your advertisement especially distinctive or use more space than usual in order to make it attract attention out of all the others competing with it for this honor. But it will be worth while.

Keep a careful list of the names and addresses of all people who write you each year and ask for your catalog or other advertising literature. These form a valuable list of prospective customers and should not be lost track of; you have paid valuable money to secure these names and they should be kept on the list until it seems that they cannot be interested in your proposition.

Be very sure to keep a list of people who have purchased goods and stock from you. These are the rocks upon which you are to erect your business structure and they should be good for repeat orders year after year if you have treated them fairly and sold them a quality product, and not overcharged them.

How to advertise presents a question that will depend entirely upon the amount of stock or eggs you have to sell. If the amount is limited, you will not be able to afford very much advertising space in marketing them. Where you are running a large plant and have a large volume to turn over, then more space will be necessary to create the demand so vital to a marketing of the product. This is a question which every individual breeder or farmer will have to settle himself, giving due reference to the products he has to sell.

Unquestionably, the most effective copy is that which occupies a space sufficiently large as to attract the maximum attention. In the average paper this will be nothing short of a full-page advertisement, but since this is out of the question in selling poultry products, we need not lose sight of the principle and discard it entirely. It still holds true.

Let us examine a few actual advertisements and note the difference they make in the attention aroused in the casual reader's eye as he glances through the paper.

This advertisement occupies "three lines" in the classified section:

EXTRA CHOICE S. C. Brown Leghorn ckls.; large size and nice dark color; $1.25 each. 6 for $7.50, $14 doz. (Name and address.)

CHAPTER XV

This is a "four line" advertisement in the same paper. Note the difference the extra line makes in the attention aroused:

S. O. White LEGHORN COCKERELS— Apnl hatched only; of Ferris trap-nested 265 to 300 eee strain; $2 each: $1.50 each for six or mor-. (Name and address.)

This is a "one inch" advertisement from the same page. Note how the extra space makes possible a different type arrangement which attracts several times the attention of the advertisement above:

*English, Barron
S. C. W. Leghorns
DIRECT DESCENDANTS from imported stock; well developed with quailty of show birds. Our herds have been tested and developed until we hatch our stock from the strongest of producers. Choice cockerels, $2.25 each; $2 in lots of six or more; $22 per doz. A few special choice show birds, $3. (Name and address.)*

This is a "two inch" adverfisement in which the outstanding offering the breeder has to make, namely "hatching eggs" and the breed, is most prominently displayed. Next in the range of the eye is the name and address, which, for obvious reasons has been omitted:

*American
S. C. W. Leghorn
Hatching Eggs
from my breeding pena of trap-nest pedigreed stock of high-scoring, high-producing birds. Prices reasonable. Place your orders early. Also eggs from range stock. (Name and address.)*

A few general suggestions as to what should enter into a good piece of advertising copy, regardless of the space it occupies, may be of service. Of course, it should be realized that certain things can best be accomplished where there is sufficient space at the disposal of the copy writer to allow a measure of freedom not generally possible with small spaces.

H. Cecil Sheppard, a specialty breeder of Aneonas, who is possibly the most conspicuously successful advertiser of all poultrymen, has a graphic way of saying just what one should attempt to do with his advertising copy. As Mr. Sheppard puts it, there are just four "L's" in the successful advertisement. They are:

Make 'em LOOK.
Make 'em LIKE.
Make 'em LEARN.
LAND 'em.

There is a world of sales and advertising wisdom tucked up in these short, terse statements. They are the meat of the experience gained by Mr. Shppard in nearly 20 years of business effort. The man who originated them is selling $100,000 worth of pure-bred poultry each year, as he has stated over his own signature, and this is but one standard by which to judge the results won by advertising properly done, for one man. A few years ago he was traveling salesman for a leather house.

Advertising cannot build a business for the man who has nothing worth while to offer. This means that there must be a service in the goods you have to sell, if permanent success is to be won. Any business deal which does not benefit both parties is immoral, and if you are not giving your customers full value for their money and a dependable article, all the advertising in the world will not save your business from the dry-rot of decay and failure.

There is an advantage in selecting a trade-mark for your product and in having it registered in the U. S. Patent Office. You can then give your goods a name or mark which you alone will be permitted to use, and which, in time, will set your goods apart from those of your competitors. And this is just as valuable to the utility or market egg breeder as to the fancier.

CHAPTER XV

A few of the trade names copyrighted and used by different market egg breeders are as follows: "Yesterlaid," "Egglantine Farms," "New-Laid Eggs," "JustLaid," "Egg-A-Day Strain," "Sunny Crest Farm."

In signing advertisements or determining how you shall conduct the business it is much better to do business as an individual, using your own name, than it is to hide behind a firm name that does not disclose an identity. It is harder to keep in mind the "Maple Grove Poultry Farm" than it is John A. Smith. People remember and like to deal with a person more than they remember or like to deal with a firm name. If you are a woman, do not hesitate to do business under "Mrs. Julia Brown" or whatever your name is, rather than picking out some common farm name which some other person may take a notion to use. No one can appropriate your name or trade upon it and the good will and prestige you build up in your advertising will flow all to you. And, as a woman, keep in mind the fact that thousands of other farm women are going to be attracted to you and send you their business largely because they feel on a common footing with you. Some of the best specialty poultry breeders in the world are women. One of the foremost poultry breeders in England is a woman and her birds are shipped all over the world.

Advertising is a great and powerful arm of modern commercial life. It has brought our entire business, and, therefore, our entire civilization, to the present high state of efficiency which it enjoys. It must be used if any great success is to be made in the poultry business. In fact, that business can never get out of the local class without the aid of advertising. This means that the science of selling by the printed page must have attention from the farmer and poultryman who has surplus stock to market. He will find it almost as fascinating a study as his work in the breeding pen.

CHAPTER XVI

Poultry Diseases and Remedies

It is very easy to acquire the belief, once disease breaks out in the flock, that fowls are not naturally hardy and are, in fact, very susceptible to disease and contagion. A more erroneous opinion could not be held in regard to the hardiness of poultry. As a matter of fact, the losses from disease the country over is not very great, although in localities outbreaks may assume the form of epidemics at times due to the long sapping of vitality through neglect, improper care or contagion.

Fowls subjected to disease attacks are not profitable in any sense of the term. Too much of the nervous energy of the fowl and too much of the ration goes to fighting these pests and organisms that ought to be going to the maintenance of flesh and the formation of eggs. A fowl afflicted with vermin, for instance, has its hands full and can be expected to do little else than hold its own.

A careful survey of poultry diseases has been made and it appears that practically every disease, an exception is found in only two or three instances, is caused through contagion rather than through any other source. This fact will afford a great tool to the poultryman or farmer in fighting disease, if he but keep it in mind. It means that if diseased fowls are destroyed as soon as their condition becomes apparent, that if every precaution is used to prevent the spread of infection even where it is not apparent, by practicing the utmost cleanliness and by constantly keeping the premises clean and disinfected, the likelihood of disease ever becoming serious in the flock is reduced to a minimum. It is where things are allowed to drag along that conditions get in a bad way— most of the flock has been infected before one takes the matter in hand.

The great object in acquainting yourself with the various common poultry diseases is not to learn how to "doctor" poultry. That method of treatment never was and probably never will be satisfactory. One cannot cure poultry diseases, in the majority of instances, in the sense that a complete recovery can be secured. In many instances a recovered diseased fowl is but a link in the breeding cycle of the germ which starts a new source of infection and movement that transmits the disease, either by contagion or through breeding, to another generation. This is particularly true in the case of white diarrhoea. It should be laid down as an absolute rule in the poultry yard that all fowls apparently cured from disease, or all fowls exposed to a disease, should not be used in the breeding yards. That is one sure way of breaking the life cycle of these deadly germ diseases.

The object of getting acquainted with the different poultry diseases is to discover what causes them and then to go about the work of preventing them. Prevention is always more satisfactory than cure, and will yield considerably more in dividends.

The very first point in the prevention of poultry disease is to start with the right kind of stock, free from disease of any kind or parasites, and keep these fowls in surroundings that are likewise free from these enemies. If the housing conditions are correct and along principles or plans making it easy to keep them in a sanitary condition, the chances of disease getting a foothold in your flock will be extremely remote. One of the compuratively recent innovations in the poultry world is the attempt being made in some states to place all hatcheries and flocks from which breeding stock, hatching eggs or baby chicks are sold under the license system in order that they may be inspected for disease and any flock found suffering from white diarrhoea or other contagious disease will not be permitted to do business.

The U. S. Department of Agriculture has this to say about the prevention of disease in the poultry yard:

"By beginning in this manner a flock may be obtained which is practically free from disease germs and parasites, but in order to keep it in this condition the premises must be frequently cleaned and occasionally disinfected. There are a number of reasons for this. First, there are certain germs generally present in the intestines of healthy fowls that are scattered with the manure, and which, when they are permitted to accumulate and become very numerous, may cause outbreaks of disease; second, the germs of contagious diseases may be brought to the poultry yard by pigeons or other birds which fly from one poultry yard to another, or by mice or rats; third, it is seldom that ground is obtained that is free from infection with the eggs of parasitic worms and the spores of disease producing microbes. To keep these germs and parasites from developing and

CHAPTER XVI

increasing their numbers to a dangerous extent the houses should be kept clean, the drinking fountains and feed troughs should be washed every week with boiling water or other disinfectant, and, if any lice or mites are found on the birds or in their houses, the roosts and adjoining parts of the walls should be painted with a mixture of kerosene, 1 quart, and crude carbolic acid or crude cresol, 1 teacup (1 gill). Or the house may be whitewashed with freshly slaked lime or sprayed with kerosene emulsion. The fowls should be dusted with lice powder."

Good disinfectants should be regularly and thoroughlyused throughout the year. They can be purchased at any poultry supply house, drug or feed store and should be on hand all the time. One can hardly overdo the work of keeping the buildings, premises and appliances sanitary and clean. This is of special importance in the seasons when disease and parasites are most apt to thrive and develop, namely in the fall months when the atmosphere is damp and during the summer when the natural heat rapidly promotes the development of germ life and the hatching of eggs of parasites.

There are a number of common poultry diseases which are found in all sections and which are most likely to occur. These should be studied in order that they may be recognized in case of infection and the proper measures applied:

Roup

Roup is a contagious catarrh attacking the membrane lining of the eye, the sacs below the eye, the nostrils, the larynx and the trachea. It is similar to influenza in man or severe colds in the head. It is always attended by fever and is an extremely highly contagious disease. In fact, it seems to be spread entirely by contagion; that is, by contact with diseased fowls or the germs coming from diseased fowls. The nature of the microbe causing it is not known at this time.

The symptoms generally start with a cold, but in the more advanced stages fever develops, sluggishness and prostration follow. The breathing becomes hard and labored and the eyes swell shut. The birds will be found sneezing and making efforts to dislodge the mucus from the breathing passages by shaking head. There is no appetite and the birds generally sit around with drooping head and closed eyes.

The treatment is to immediately isolate the affected fowls from the rest of the flock by placing them in a. dry, warm and well-ventilated room free from drafts. Antiseptic mixtures are applied to the mucous membranes either with a small syringe or oil can, or the bird's head may be plunged in a bowl of the mixture and held there a few seconds. The remedies recommended for such treatment are:

Boric acid, 1 ounce; water 1 quart.

Or, permanganate of potash, 1 dram; water, 1 pint.

Or, boric acid, 1 1/4 ounces; borate of soda, 1/2 ounce; water, 1 quart.

Or, peroxide of hydrogen, 1 ounce; water, 3 ounces.

After this treatment anoint the head with pure vaseline or camphorated vaseline.

If the disease is of a severe type, the best remedy is to destroy the whole flock and burn the carcasses, thoroughly disinfected the houses and premises before introducing new stock. This may, in the long run, be the most profitable method because it will get away from the possibility of any infected birds, or birds containing the germs getting into the breeding pens or in contact with the young stock and infecting the next generation.

Diphtheria

Diphtheria starts with the symptoms of a cold like roup, but differs from it and is distinguished from it by the development of false membranes on the mucous surface of the nostrils, eyes, mouth, throat and smaller air tubes.

It is a strictly contagious disease and it is thought that it never develops as a result of exposure to cold or dampness, although once it gets a start it is recognized that these conditions favor its development.

There is no satisfactory treatment for diphtheria and the best plan is to kill the infected birds and burn their carcasses. The premises and houses should be thoroughly disinfected and the whole course of the disease cheeked, even if the entire flock has to be sacrificed.

CHAPTER XVI

Chicken Pox

Chicken pox or bird pox is distinguishable by an eruption of nodules on the comb, wattles and ear lobes, of irregular size ranging up to the size of a pea. Investigation on the part of experts has revealed the fact that it comes from a virus identical with that of diphtheria. This disease is spread entirely by contagion, that is, from bird to bird, and may be carried from flock to flock by birds or pigeons.

It is not a serious disease, as a rule, and may be cured by local treatment, using carbolated ointment, glycerin or oil directly on the nodules to soften the crusts. After an hour or two these preparations are removed by washing with warm water containing a little soap. The exposed tissue is then treated with a 5 per cent solution of carbolic acid, or boric acid or tincture of iodine. All founts, troughs and dishes, as well as the houses should be thoroughly disinfected in order to prevent its spread.

Cholera

Fowl cholera is a highly contagious disease spreading rapidly through a flock and is usually marked by high mortality. The very first symptom to look for is a yellowish discoloration of that part of the excrement secreted by the kidneys which is nearly perfectly white in healthy fowls. This is soon followed by diarrhoea, consisting of whitish or yellowish secretions mixed with considerable thin mucus. There is a high fever and the bird loses all interest in life, drooping about and appearing sleepy. It has no appetite, but the thirst increases, and the combs and wattles may be a dark-bluish red in color, or pale and bloodless on account of congested internal organs.

Cholera works fast and may destroy an entire flock within a week. It may apparently disappear, occasionally only killing a bird, and then break out again in serious form. Post-mortem examination reveals a swollen spleen, enlarged liver, a heart with red spots on the surface.

There is no treatment for this disease, save the killing and burning of the fowls. Be very careful in killing fowls that the blood does not get on the premises, as it contains large numbers of the germs and will spread the disease. The drinking water can be made antiseptic by adding 1 dram of permanganate of potash to each gallon of water.

Typhoid

Very similar to cholera and the same treatment advised for cholera applies here. It generally starts with drowsiness followed by prostration, which may last up to two days. The liver is enlarged, dark in color- and covered with minute necrotic spots.

White Diarrhoea

White diarrhoea is caused by four different kinds of infection and it is not worth while to enter into a detailed study of them all, except in a general way, in a work of this kind. The most common form comes from hens that have previously been infected with the disease and apparently recovered, being used in the breeding pens. This causes an organism to remain in the reproductive organs of these hens which infects the eggs they lay and these, in turn, hatch chicks having the germs in them when they are hatched. Generally the symptoms develop within a few days after the chick is hatched and the majority die hy the time they are a week to 10 days old. The contagion is also spread from chick to chick through contact and the droppings. Baby chicks are most susceptible to the disease the first 24 hours and are generally insusceptible after the fourth day, although it may appear in chicks contaminated through the droppings when the chicks are from one to two weeks old.

There is no treatment for white diarrhoea. The chicks must be killed and burned immediately upon giving indications of the disease, such as being pasted up behind. Thoroughly disinfect the water and feed troughs and change the litter of the chicks every day, if it has appeared. Give the chicks sour milk or buttermilk to drink, as it may tend to defeat its spread.

As for preventive measures, the following advice is offered by the U. S. Department of Agriculture:

"The preventive measures should begin with the eggs used for hatching. If these are purchased, they should be accepted only from flocks known to be healthy and the eggs of which give rise to healthy chicks. If this assurance cannot be obtained, it is better to produce the eggs needed for hatching on the home farm and from hens that are known to be free from infection.

"Having obtained the eggs, they should be kept until ready for incubation in a dry, moderately cool place, so spread out that the air can circulate over them and carry away the moisture which they exhale. They should not be placed in hay, straw, chaff or other substance liable to be musty or moldy. Before putting them into the incubator or under the hen they should be wiped with a cloth wet in grain alcohol of 70 or 80 per cent strength to remove any germs that might be on the outside of the shell. The hens used for hatching should be free from all infection, and the incubator should be thoroughly cleaned. If there have been any sick chicks in it, it should be thoroughly disinfected by washing with compound solution of cresol (5 per cent solution). The same precautions should be adopted in regard to the brooder."

Tuberculosis

This is a chronic contagious disease which develops nodules or tubercles in various organs of the body, but generally in the liver, spleen and intestines. The most frequent place is in the liver, and a post mortem examination should soon reveal whether or not tuberculosis is responsible for the fowl's death. It is highly contagious and readily communicated from fowl to fowl. It generally is pretty well distributed throughout the flock before the attendant is aware of its presence at all.

The symptoms begin with gradual loss of weight, wasting of muscles, paleness of comb and, near the end, sleepiness and diarrhea. It often causes inflammation and swelling in the joints producing lameness, which, in many instances, is the first outward symptom the poultryman or farmer has as to the presence of the disease.

There is no treatment for tuberculosis. The fowls affected must be destroyed and burned, and it will save money in the long run to kill off the whole flock, burn them, and thoroughly disinfect the houses, appliances and premises. No attempt should be made to save any of the fowls. Those apparently all right are, in truth, suffering from diseased livers and will only prove a breeding ground for the bacilli causing the disease.

Intestinal Worms

Fowls affected with intestinal worms can generally be detected by their light weight and weakness. If one cares to kill them and make an examination of the intestines, the thin white worms can be discovered by mixing the contents with water in a dark-colored pan.

The following treatment is suggested by the California Experiment Station:

"For 100 birds, steep one pound of finely chopped tobacco stems for two hours in water enough to cover them. Mix the stems and the liquid with one-half the usual ration of ground feed. The day previous to treatment withhold all feed, giving water only. After the birds have been starved for 24 hours, feed the medicated mash, and two hours after it is cleaned up give them one-fourth of the usual ration of ground feed mixed with water in which Epsom salt has been dissolved at the rate of 11 ounces for each 100 birds. The treatment should be repeated 10 days later."

In the case of tapeworms a slightly different treatment must be given. The Bureau of Animal Industry, U. S. Department of Agriculture, states that a number of different treatments have been tried, none of which proved very successful. "A few worms may be eliminated by dozing each bird with a teaspoonful of castor oil to which has been added from 19 to 20 drops of oil of shenopodium (American wormseed oil), according to the weight of the bird. The medicine should be given after a fast and repeated again in 10 days. If the medicinal treatment is combined with measures to maintain the surroundings in a clean and sanitary condition, including good drainage and removal of the manure and other litter, infestation with tapeworms is less likely to cause serious trouble than if these precautions are neglected."

Limberneck

This is not a disease in itself but generally a symptom of several other diseases characterized by a paralysis of the neck, which causes the fowl to lose control of its head so that it cannot raise it up from the ground. This is due to the absorption of poisons from the intestines, acting upon the nervous system and causing paralysis.

Use a strong purgative such as 50 to 60 grains of Epsom salt or 3 or 4 teaspoonfuls of castor oil for a grown fowl and they will generally be all right in 24 hours. If not better in two or three days, it is best to kill them.

Scaly Legs

Minute parasites burrowing under the scales on the legs cause scaly leg. This is not, in the early stages, a serious or painful trouble, but if it is allowed to go it will soon practically reduce the fowl to a state of inactivity. It is easily recognized by the enlargement of the legs and feet due to the crusts thrown up by the parasites.

The first step in treating it is to paint the roosts and dropping boards with wood preservative or crude petroleum as a precautionary measure against the further spreading of the disease. Then wash the feet in soap and warm water until the scales are loosened and come off. Only those harboring parasites will do this. Then apply an ointment containing a 2 per cent carbolic acid or the sulphur ointment or a mixture of Peruvian balsam, 1 ounce and alcohol, 3 ounces. Carbolated vaseline is also good.

Lice, Mites

It is not economical, as a rule, to attempt to mix home insecticides and disinfectants. These can be purchased at any feed, seed or drug store at a very economical price. The best plan in fighting mites or lice is to buy these commercial sprays or powders and apply them in the manner suggested by the manufacturer.

A good disinfectant, in addition to liquid louse killer, should be kept in hand at all times for the purpose of spraying as a preventative against the outbreak or spread of diseases among the flock.

www.ingramcontent.com/pod-product-compliance
Lightning Source LLC
Chambersburg PA
CBHW031623210526
45464CB00004B/1725